Our Favorite Chinese Menus

Chinese Appetizer Party

Shrimp Toast
Fried Won-Tons
Tea Eggs
Oyster Cakes
Barbecued Spareribs
Stuffed Mushroom Caps
Bacon-Wrapped Water Chestnuts
Sizzled Noodle Shreds

Gala Chinese Dinner
for Eight or Ten

Cantonese Egg Rolls
Won-Ton Soup
Fried Rice, Canton or Rice
Sweet-and-Sour Shrimp
Chicken Stir-Fried with Walnuts
Chinese Mushrooms, Snow Peas, and
    Bamboo Shoots
Date Won-Tons or Fruit

Chinese Patio Dinner for Eight

Sweet-and-Sour Meat Balls
Chop Suey Chimney Hill
Shrimp Fried Rice
Crisped Marinated Celery
Chilled Pineapple and Honeydew
    Melon

Chinese Patio Dinner for Six

Bird's Nest Soup
Pork Chow Mein with Shrimp
Sweet-and-Sour Carrots
Sliced Cold Radish
Honeyed Apples or Fruit

Chinese Patio Dinner for Six

Shrimp with Bamboo Shoots,
    Szechwan

Chicken Fried Rice
Spinach and Mushrooms
Lichee Nuts (canned)

Budget Chinese Dinner for Eight

Sour-and-Hot Soup
Sizzling Rice Patties
Sweet-and-Sour Fish
Hamburger and Mushrooms with
    Scallions
Rice
Almond Cookies

Chinese Dinner for Six

Shrimp Balls, China
Green Beans, Fukien
Chicken Lo Mein   Rice
Peking Dust

Easy Chinese Dinner for Four

Egg Drop Soup
Beef Shreds Stir-Fried with Onions
Celery Stir-Fried with Fresh
    Mushrooms
Rice
Chilled Crushed Pineapple (canned)

Chinese Dinner for Two

Lobster with Black Beans, Canton
Rice
Cold and Spicy Celery
Bananas in a Candy Coat

Fast Chinese Luncheon for
Two or Four

Won-Ton Soup or Egg Drop Soup
Fu Yung with Shrimp
Fortune Cookies

Oriental Cooking
the Fast Wok Way

Oriental Cooking
the Fast Wok Way

by Jacqueline Hériteau

A Helen Van Pelt Wilson Book

HAWTHORN BOOKS, INC.
Publishers
New York

ORIENTAL COOKING THE FAST WOK WAY

Drawings by Edward Epstein

For our three
mini-gourmets—
Kris, David, and Holly

Contents

List of Illustrations

The Egg Roll and I

We have a passion for egg rolls.

More accurately, I have a passion for egg rolls, and David shared a stint in the Air Force with Wu Kung, who taught him how good *good* Chinese food can be. Our pooled interests, mine in a recipe for egg rolls, and David's in egg rolls and all Chinese food, led us on a quest for good Chinese recipes.

It might have ended there, but when we tasted a Japanese sukiyaki dinner, we decided we had to include recipes from any country where *wok* cooking prevails. Then, at the home of an Indian friend, we ran into a *korma* curry, and it was so fantastically good and different that we knew we had to investigate the cooking of countries where curry is used.

To learn even a little about these two great schools, flash-cooking and curry-cooking, is to become a fan. The methods are super-simple. No soufflés to fall, sauces to ruin, special utensils to clutter the kitchen. You can cook most, if not quite all, of the best things out of doors, even on a boat, over a few sticks of kindling. Many Eastern families still do. The kitchen battery need include only a cleaver, a chopping area, a *wok* or skillet, a spatula, a sieve, and a pot or two. The diet is a remarkably healthy one—nutrients are never destroyed by overcooking, nor are they leeched out by boiling and then discarded with the water—and inexpensive, too, even luxury dishes. You use only a little of the costly items such as meat and seafood to achieve exotic flavors and nutritious meals.

But what we admire and enjoy perhaps most of all is the extraordinary diversity Eastern cooks achieve with simple ingredients. I have selected here 150 recipes that we particularly like and find for the greater part fast, easy, and accessible in terms of ingredients. (A few are included for other reasons, primarily to make it possible to put together fairly complete meals of one country or another.) But I have read, tried, and tasted hundreds more, and have acquired boundless admiration for the sophistication, subtlety, and sheer good taste of Oriental cuisine.

Egg rolls are not a unique and accidental *delight* of Oriental cooking: it's *all* that good. We hope you develop a passion for egg rolls, too.

J. H.
Sharon, Connecticut

Oriental Cooking the Fast Wok Way

I. The Way and the Wok

THE RECIPES in this book come from more than a dozen countries and regions of the Far East. The majority of the recipes, those *without* the name of the country of origin attached to them, are Chinese and are flash-cooked. Another group is Vietnamese and similar in preparation. The Japanese recipes given are specialties such as Sashimi (raw fish), Sukiyaki (meat and vegetables flash-cooked in broth), and Vinegared Rice.

The second largest group of recipes is from India and is curry-cooking. A handful are from countries such as Malaysia and Java where curry-cooking also prevails. In planning Far Eastern menus, draw on the Chinese collection for extra dishes to serve with Japanese or Vietnamese meals. The Indian group will provide extras and accessories to serve with the spicy, aromatic curry foods of other countries.

Traditionally in China and India, meals are not presented in courses as they are in the West. At family meals in China a small bowl of plain rice is set before each place with chopsticks, which are used to pick up morsels from the communal main dishes set in the center of the table. A small porcelain spoon is used to dip from the communal soup tureen. All the main dishes, including soup, sweet, and appetizer, are set out at the same time. At banquets, a thimble-sized cup of warm wine is set beside each rice bowl, and the main dishes troop in throughout the meal—soups, appetizers, sweets, meats, everything.

In India, as in China, it has been the general custom to serve all the components of a meal at once rather than in a sequence of courses. If any order is observed, the sweet comes first. Customs vary somewhat from region to region.

The Way

It is important to understand not only that the following recipes are nice and fast, but that they *have to be fast* to be nice, with the exception of the curries. Flash-cooking is the *way*, the key to the flavors and textures we associate with Far Eastern food. Ingredients are cut to bite-sized bits, measured, assembled by the stove, tossed in timed sequence into a little searing-hot shortening, and stirred and fried, usually no more than 3 to 8 minutes. It isn't exactly frantic, but it is fast.

The *wok*, all-purpose cooking utensil of China (and some neighboring countries around), makes flash-cooking easy. *Woks* are inexpensive and can be found in shops specializing in Oriental gifts and foods. But a *wok* isn't necessary to *wok* cookery. A large heavy skillet or an electric skillet (preferably round) will do almost as well, though it isn't nearly so much fun.

Instructions for cutting, measuring, and other preparations of all the ingredients are given in the first paragraphs of each recipe. I place prepared ingredients on sheets of wax paper (to save the dishwasher), or in custard cups or bowls, and set them by the stove in the order in which they are listed, which is also the order in which they will be added to the *wok*. It's pretty obvious, since the whole thing will be cooked in about 5 minutes, that there won't be time, once you start, to stop and chop something.

As soon as an ingredient goes into the *wok*, I toss it so that all the pieces are seared in the oil; then with a spatula or

Wok

spoon I keep the slices moving rapidly over the hot metal surfaces. They will wilt and become translucent in a minute or two. Then their natural color will intensify and eventually become even more intense. That's when they should come out. Even if they still seem a little raw, they will finish cooking in their own heat. If vegetables stay in long enough to loose their color, they will be overcooked. Times given for cooking are indications; your eye is the best judge of the exact moment when a food is finished.

The recipe tag line: "Serves 4, more if other dishes are offered," means that the specified amount of ingredients will make four Western-style portions, more if the dish is part of a multi-dish Oriental meal, in which smaller portions are offered.

Many Chinese recipes end with the addition of cornstarch dissolved in water, a thickener that binds the juices in the pan. If it lumps in the *wok*, add a tablespoon or two of water, just enough to smooth it out. The sauce isn't supposed to be a bath, just a glaze.

Deep-frying, another common method of cooking in China, is discussed in the introduction to Chapter 3. The Chinese do, of course, broil, bake, roast, as we do, but this is a collection of recipes for flash *wok* cooking.

The Cutting

Cutting and chopping in the Chinese style is an art.

The size and shape of ingredients govern the time they will need to cook. You don't have to be a chopping-block artist to flash-cook, but to flash-cook successfully you do have to cut as recipes direct. The names of the cuts are special, but only one is really different—roll-cutting—and it's intriguing. Here they are:

Roll-out diagonals are cuts used for celery, green beans, and other long tubular vegetables. Place the vegetable straight in

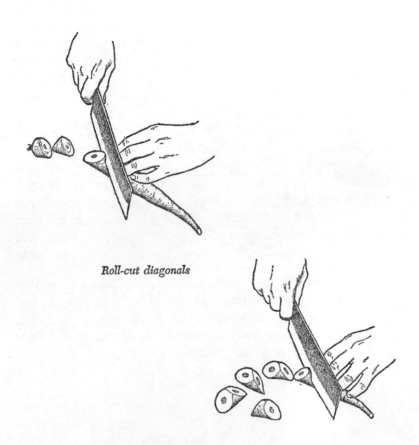

Roll-cut diagonals

front of you, turn the knife at a diagonal, cut, then roll the vegetable over 180 degrees, that is, onto its other side; with the knife at the same angle as before, cut again. And keep cutting in this way. The pieces will be roughly triangular in shape, and will expose a great deal of the interior of the vegetable. Roll-cut shapes are easy to stir-fry since they won't stick to each other or the pan, and the exposure of a large portion of the interior allows tougher vegetables to cook more quickly.

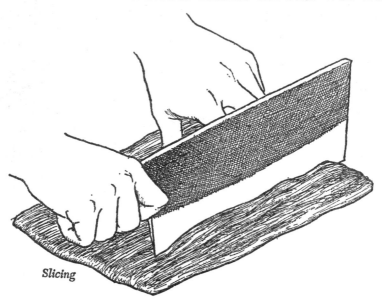

Slicing

Sliced means cutting meat, fish, or vegetables into thin strips, 2 inches long by 1 inch wide by ¼ to ⅛ inch thick. Cut meats with the grain into strips. Then cut across the grain. This makes them more tender. Freeze soft ingredients slightly before attempting very thin slices.

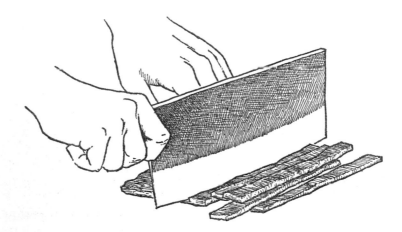

Shreds are cuts to 1 to 2 inches long, ⅛ inch wide, and ⅛ inch thick (or as close to that as you can get). I haven't the patience to do hard vegetables, such as turnips, this way, and sometimes I cheat and shred them on the coarse side of a grater.

Diced means cut into cubes ¼ to ½ inch square.

Cubed means cut into larger cubes, about 1 inch square.

Chopped means cut coarsely into bits. A blender at low speed chops admirably such things as onions and frozen shrimp. Cut large pieces into chunks before placing them in the blender.

Minced means chopped as fine as possible. Set the blender at high.

Smashed (usually garlic) means hit hard enough to expose the interior.

Crushed means pressed through a garlic crusher or crushed with a knife point.

The *Wok*

The *wok's* great advantage is the flare of its sides, which tends to keep morsels tumbled into the little well of shortening at the bottom of the *wok*, so that more searing gets done with less shortening. And since these broad sides become as hot, and even hotter than, the bottom of the pot, there's a lot of room on which to sizzle the seared ingredients.

Wok accessories that are particularly useful include a cover, a Chinese spatula (I also use a slotted spoon) for stirring, a

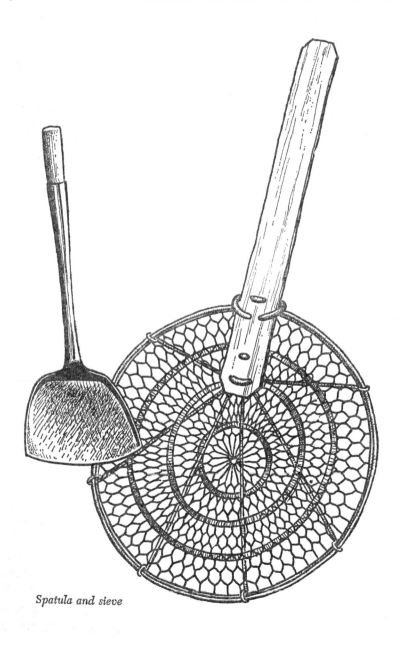

Spatula and sieve

Chinese sieve for removing lots of ingredients from oil at one swoop (it's decorative, too), a 3-inch-wide cleaver. A large French knife cuts as well, but the Chinese cleaver's broad sides are useful for picking up and transferring cut materials.

Steam baskets are available for use with a *wok,* but steaming is slow, and you may not want to use a steamer often enough to make buying the basket worthwhile. The important thing to know about steaming is this: Recipes mean *wet-steamed,* not double-boiled. One way to substitute for a steam basket is to steam ingredients on an ovenproof dish set on custard cups in a large pan that has a lid, a roasting pan for instance, with water in the bottom.

Woks are sold with round metal bases that adapt them to modern stoves. On a Chattie, a little round stove commonly used for cooking in earlier times, the adapter obviously wasn't necessary. To use the *wok,* set the metal base over the burner so that it rests solidly, then set the *wok* on the ring. That's all there is to it.

Woks come in several sizes. I use two *woks* to cook dinners for eight. Aluminum *woks* may be easiest to find, but the one I prefer is a 14-inch *wok* of sheet or cold-pressed metal (I think), from Taiwan. It has a primitive look, cooks more successfully, and handles more food. My 12-inch aluminum *wok* cooks (properly) only enough food to serve two or three persons.

Most of the imported *woks* have to be "seasoned." (I seasoned the aluminum *wok* too, but that didn't seem to do anything much to it one way or another.) Some *woks* are sold with a protective coating to prevent rust, and this should be rubbed off gently with steel wool. To season the *wok,* once its gray protective coating is removed, heat it until it's sizzling hot and rub the inside all over with a pad soaked in oil. It will smoke mightily. Remove it to the sink, spray with hot water, and repeat the process twice more. In time, the *wok* will be all black, inside and out, beautifully seasoned, and nothing will stick to it. Wash your *wok* only in water. If foods cook dry or cornstarch sticks, soak it clean.

The *Wok* and Your Stove

Gas stoves, which give greater and closer heat control, are most practical for *wok* cookery, but an electric stove works, too. Just make sure the burner is at high heat before you place the *wok* over it and that the *wok* itself has become sizzling hot before you add the oil. Don't use a *wok* without its adapter ring on an electric burner. The bottom will overheat, the sides will underheat, and everything will cook unevenly. If the *wok* gets too hot when you are using it on an electric stove, lift it off for a second and turn down the heat.

Oriental Cooking out of Doors

The *wok* owes its origin probably, and its popularity certainly, to historic fuel shortages that made fast cooking with little fuel essential. So that makes the *wok* a great cook-out utensil. A Chattie, the portable cone-shaped stove with a circular opening at the top, would be nice to have to cook outdoors, but a Japanese hibachi works very well with a *wok*, and we use a conventional barbecue grill (with the adapter ring), too.

When cooking with the *wok* on a barbecue or an hibachi, we heat a small mound of briquettes to glowing, spread them slightly, and place on top of them a few sticks of thin, dry kindling. When the kindling flames and the *wok* is hot enough to sizzle a drop of water, we add the oil and cook.

Indian cooking on the patio is different, with or without a *wok*. Curries are cooked more slowly than flash-fried foods, so we start them several inches above a medium pile of glowing briquettes. Since kebabs are part of the Indian dinner scene, we take advantage of larger grills to start a batch of kebabs on skewers at about the time the curry dish is half done.

Any of the one-dish dinners you'll find in this book, and in the menu suggestions, will make a great cook-out meal. Do the rice indoors, earlier.

Choosing a Menu

Planning an Oriental menu takes quite a lot of thought if you're not an Oriental.

Indian-style meals consist of curry, rice, which may be plain boiled or a flavored *pulao,* and various little side dishes containing condiments and chutney. A soup, vegetable, kebabs, and meat dishes may also be served with unleavened or fried bread. Dessert is in order. Beer is a suitable beverage—or a chilled white wine such as Chablis, or even a dry rosé. Tea with milk and sugar is a correct beverage to serve with curry meals. If there are to be cocktails, gin-based cocktails work best.

When planning Chinese-style meals for more than two, I usually select three main dishes, one primarily meat, one fish, one vegetable, and serve these with plain boiled rice. For contrast I like to include one sweet-and-sour dish and one fried dish. Fried rice, which can be made beforehand and warmed, is a handy choice for company dinners. Begin with an appetizer followed by a soup and end with a sweet, or set it all on the table at the same time, along with soy sauce and Sweet-and-Sour Sauce, unless one of the dishes is a sweet-and-sour dish. Warm rice wine by the thimbleful is the correct beverage. Beer works well, too. We prefer a chilled, light white wine. We also like China tea after Chinese meals, and put a little sugar into the pot.

You'll find some dinner menu suggestions on the inside of the front and back covers. Use Chinese recipes to round out menus for Vietnamese and Japanese meals—and Indian foods to complete menus for meals from other curry-cooking lands.

Oriental Diet

When you have absolutely had that crash diet, relax it a little by calorie-counting the Chinese or Japanese way.

In point of fact, the Chinese do not need to calorie-count at all—or hardly, as their food is practically already a diet. They eat more vegetables than animal foods (which contain a lot of fat), and more green vegetables and starchless vegetables than we do. As for fats, meats used are mostly lean, and the amount of oil (polyunsaturated) used is minimal and can be halved.

Desserts are not a necessity to Chinese meals either, and those we are accustomed to having in restaurants are usually very low in sugar, as, for instance, Fortune Cookies. One rarely feels the need for a sweet after an Oriental meal, and is usually content to top it off with a cup of light, almost sugarless tea. You can calorie-count by skipping the rice that accompanies Chinese meals, too, though you will want to serve some form of *pasta* or rice to the other members of the family who need these energy-giving starches.

Dinners *à la chinoise* are also a great way to entertain friends while you diet, or to entertain dieting friends. When guests are many, you will need several dishes to offer if everyone is going to avoid the rice. Make one or two yourself, and fill in with canned or frozen packaged foods from the supermarket.

A few calorie-conscious recipes are given in the last chapter. They are not my top favorites, but they are good, and you might like to try them even if you are not on a diet.

2. Secrets of an Oriental Larder

WITH A HANDFUL of dried and frozen ingredients and left-over odds and ends, you can make, or improvise upon, many kinds of Chinese dishes. Last night, for instance, David balked at the prospect of hamburger, American-style (I was typing), so—I put oil into the big *wok*, stir-fried in it the hamburger with chopped onion, added a tag end of chopped cabbage, some celery leaves (all I had left), some tired mushrooms I found at the back of the crisper, leftover water chestnuts, and perhaps 8 frozen raw shrimp, chopped. The flavorings were a slice of fresh ginger, soy sauce, oyster sauce, sugar, and salt. It was great, and took about 15 minutes, including chopping and cooking.

Some ingredients from our potluck supper may sound exotic as stock for the larder, but they are no more difficult and scarcely more expensive to keep on hand than staples of the American larder.

With just soy sauce and the ingredients you have on hand now, you can cook a surprising number of Oriental dishes, but after a while you may tire of the similarity of flavor the dishes will have. So it's worthwhile investing in some supermarket extras and in a few of the imports sold by specialty shops (listed at the end of this book). These extras will add diversity and distinction to your Oriental repertoire. The list to consider is long, but only a handful are items you really need and will use regularly.

There are also a few ingredients it is handy to know how to make, either because you may run out of store equivalents or because they are better when homemade. Chicken Stock (use the Fast Chicken Stock recipe) is foremost. Sweet-and-Sour Sauce and Chutney are nice to homemake, too.

Along with things you buy or make, consider your stock of leftovers—they have great potential in this type of cooking. Lots of recipes call for cooked pork, some for cooked chicken. Fried rices are made with leftover rice, and Chow Mein with leftover (or at least cooked) noodles. Tag ends of roasts and raw vegetables can be very useful. Drippings from pork roasts and fat from Chicken Stock are excellent substitutes for oil in cooking, particularly for vegetables. When you open a package of frozen peas, save a few to give color to some future Chinese dish. With leftovers, a few of the items below, an egg or two, Egg-Roll and Won-Ton Wrappers in the freezer, there's hardly a recipe in this book that you can't make on the spur of the moment.

Basics from Your Market

The backbone of the larder:

BAMBOO SHOOTS: Sold canned in supermarkets. Rinse and crisp before using. Store covered with water in refrigerator. Whole fresh shoots are sold in specialty shops, but are harder to prepare.

BEAN SPROUTS: You can grow your own from mung beans in the kitchen, but the canned product, crisped, is fine, and lots easier. Store covered with water in the refrigerator. Rinse well before using.

CABBAGE: Chinese celery and cabbage are sold in specialty shops and are easy to grow in your backyard if they are not available locally. Plain cabbage is a fine substitute in most recipes. One head lasts forever in the crisper.

CANNED PINEAPPLE: Tidbits in syrup, and chunks in juices, unsweetened, are used in various sweet-and-sour sauces. Nice as dessert for Oriental meals, too.

CELERY: Turns up in lots of recipes for texture as well as flavor.

DRY SHERRY: Portuguese brands are nice. Rice wine is the authentic ingredient and is sold in specialty shops. I think that sherry is just as good.

GARLIC: Garlic powder is a poor substitute. Use ½ teaspoon of powder to replace 1 clove. Peel cloves before using.

GINGER: Fresh ginger is best, and is sold at Chinese and Puerto Rican greengrocers. Keeps frozen or refrigerated for months. Substitute ½ teaspoon of ground for 1 teaspoon of fresh. Don't peel before using. (The vitamins are in the peel, I firmly believe, and I never peel vegetables, or hardly ever.)

MUSHROOMS: Ditto. If they are withering, slice lengthwise, sauté very lightly in a bit of oil, freeze, and use later.

MUSTARD SAUCES: Can be purchased or homemade. See page 22.

OIL: I prefer a light corn oil to peanut oil. Refrigerate after opening.

PORK: Keep handy. Called for as a flavoring as well as main ingredient. Buy lean cuts, have them ground, and store packed into 1-cup lots in the freezer. Store some in 1-pound lots, too, un-ground. Save tag ends of roasts, minced, in half-cup lots, frozen.

SCALLIONS (GREEN ONIONS): Peel outer skin of scallion, and use all the white and all the green that is fresh. You can substitute white onions.

SESAME SEEDS: Used for texture and flavor. Sold at the spice counter. Toasted, generally, before use.

SHRIMP: Keep handy. Packages of 21 ounces, raw, shelled, deveined, are sold in frozen-food departments. Green shrimp sold in their shells are not really more economical.

SNOW PEAS: Sold frozen in some supermarkets, and fresh at specialty shops. Grow your own: A neighbor did and said she sold them for three dollars a pound in New York last summer. A poor substitute is the flat Italian green bean.

SOY SAUCE: Seasoning most used in Chinese cooking (does amazing things to dull sauces, to Western-style gravies, too, and salads). Japanese equivalent, *shoyu*, is offered in supermarkets, and the brand I find most readily is Kikkoman. Imported soy sauce sold in specialty shops is stronger than domestic, so be wary in using it.

SPICES: Some you may not now have on your shelf, and which appear in curry cooking regularly are: coriander, cumin, aniseed, turmeric (ground), cardamom (peel and use small dark seeds), ginger powder, and curry powder, which is a mixture of these and other spices, not a spice in itself.

SUGAR: Use white, excepting for sweet-and-sour sauces.

SWEET-AND-SOUR SAUCE: Also Duck and Plum Sauce. Both are sold in supermarkets. Or you can make your own from the recipe on page 22.

WATER CHESTNUTS: Round as a chestnut, but white and crisp. Kohlrabi, which you can grow in your garden, is a good substitute. Canned water chestnuts are sold in supermarkets. Rinse before using. Store covered with water in the refrigerator.

To Order from Specialty Shops

Basics you will use often:

DRIED CHINESE MUSHROOMS: Important in many recipes, they have a flavor of their own which fresh mushrooms cannot replace. Store in an airtight container.

EGG-ROLL WRAPPERS: Make your own, or preferably order from a specialty shop and keep handy in the freezer. Shanghai wrappers are nicest but more fragile after freezing.

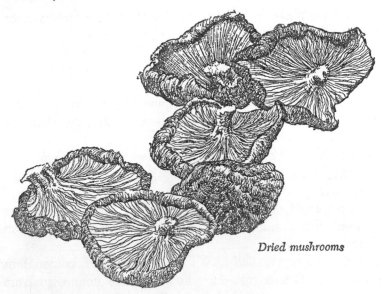

Dried mushrooms

Fɪsʜ Sᴀᴜᴄᴇ, ᴏʀ Nᴜᴏᴄ Mᴀᴍ: Vietnam's variation of the all-round seasoning.

Oʏsᴛᴇʀ Sᴀᴜᴄᴇ: Made from oysters, brine, soy sauce. No substitute, but compensate with extra soy sauce to taste. Keep stored in refrigerator after opening.

Sᴇsᴀᴍᴇ Sᴇᴇᴅ Oɪʟ: Oil used as a flavoring often with raw vegetables. Store in refrigerator after opening.

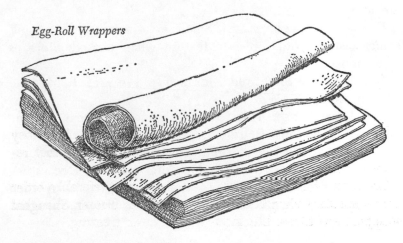

Egg-Roll Wrappers

WON-TON WRAPPERS: Tiny thin wrappers to make yourself or order. Much better to order. Keep handy in freezer.

You may use these occasionally:

BIRD'S NESTS: Whole nests or sheets made of gelatinous material with which swifts build nests in the South Seas. A gala ingredient for an occasion.

BLACK BEANS: Preserved soy beans, which accord well with some fish dishes. Store in refrigerator and add oil if they begin to dry. Good for about 6 months.

CELLOPHANE NOODLES OR BEAN THREAD: Thin beautiful noodles made from mung beans. Store in dry place. Substitute thinnest vermicelli.

CHINESE PARSLEY: The leaves and stems of coriander. Your coriander seeds will grow in a flower pot or in the garden if you keep them watered. Special flavor. I substitute celery leaves.

DRIED SHRIMP: Marvelous to look at through a glass canister and rather useful. Flavor is a cross between ham and smoked fish with shrimp overtones. Store in airtight container.

FIVE SPICE POWDER: Anise, fennel, clove, Szechwan pepper, and cinnamon in a Chinese mix. Substitute allspice.

FRESH EGG NOODLES: Make your own. Or use dried, which are almost as good.

FUNGUS OR CLOUD EARS: Small gelatinous dried fungus, rather tasteless but fun as a texture when cooked. Store as dried mushrooms.

HOISIN SAUCE: Sweet reddish sauce sold in cans. Refrigerate after opening.

RED BEAN PASTE: Thick sweet paste made from red soy beans. Sold in cans. Refrigerate after opening.

STAR ANISE: Licorice-flavored spice. Substitute aniseed.

TIGER LILY BUDS: Also called Golden Needles. Decorative, and with a flavor rather like pineapple. Useful to toss in when you want to glamorize something. Store in airtight container.

CHICKEN STOCK

5 pounds chicken and
chicken parts
4 quarts cold water

2 slices fresh ginger ½ inch
thick or 1 teaspoon
ground
1 scallion in 1-inch lengths
1 teaspoon soy sauce

1. Place chicken and water in a large kettle with ginger and scallion. Bring to a boil. Skim surface until foam stops forming. Cover, simmer over low heat 2 hours.

2. Allow to cool, remove chicken, add soy sauce, and pour clear stock into glass containers and refrigerate.

3. When fat has hardened, remove, and cover each jar. Stock will keep a week or more, and can be frozen in 1-cup lots.

Makes about 3 quarts.

FAST CHICKEN STOCK

I found after much experimenting that a brand of bland chicken granules called Steero is the most successful commercial chicken stock. Others tend to be too salty.

1 level teaspoon granules
1 cup water
½ teaspoon white vinegar
¼ teaspoon sugar

Small pinch ground ginger
2–3 drops soy sauce
½ teaspoon brandy
(optional)

Combine everything but brandy in a small saucepan and simmer for 1 minute. If stock is to be used as soup, add the brandy.

Makes 1 cup.

BEEF STOCK

I use Steero beef granules for this.

1 level teaspoon granules	Grated black pepper
1 cup water	½ teaspoon brandy
⅛ teaspoon MSG	(optional)

Combine everything but the brandy in a small saucepan and bring to simmer for 1 minute. If stock is to be used as soup, add the brandy.

Makes 1 cup.

WON-TON WRAPPERS

2 cups sifted all-purpose	1 large egg
flour	½ cup water
½ teaspoon salt	

1. Combine flour and salt in a bowl. Make a well in center of the bowl. Combine egg and water, and pour into the flour. Use your fingers to combine ingredients—it's easier. When well mixed and all the flour is absorbed, cover with a towel and allow to rest 20 minutes to 1 hour.

2. Divide dough in half. Flour the counter. Roll out the halves, giving the dough a half-turn occasionally to keep the bottom well floured. Roll dough into sheets about 12 inches square, and cut these into squares 3½ inches or less for the wrappers. They should be as thin as you can make them without tearing the dough. Don't pile to store, as they will stick together.

Makes about 3 dozen.

Cutting Won-Ton Wrappers

EGG-ROLL WRAPPERS

Make as Won-Ton Wrappers, but make the batter with ¾ cup cold water.

Roll and cut into 7-inch squares.

Should make about 16.

SWEET-AND-SOUR SAUCE

A simple version is this one:

1 tablespoon cornstarch	3 tablespoons sugar
3 tablespoons water	2 tablespoons vinegar
2 tablespoons soy sauce	1 tablespoon ketchup

Mix cornstarch and water in a custard cup. Mix soy sauce, sugar, vinegar, and ketchup in a small saucepan and bring to a simmer. Add cornstarch mixture and simmer until it thickens and clears, stirring constantly. If too thick, thin with water.

Makes about ½ cup.

A richer version is this:

½ cup chutney	1 tablespoon sugar
½ cup plum jam	1 tablespoon vinegar
¼ cup cold water	

Combine ingredients in a small saucepan, simmer 1 minute. Cool, store in refrigerator.

Makes about 1½ cups.

MUSTARD SAUCE

This is a hot one.

2 tablespoons mustard	¼ teaspoon salt
4 tablespoons cold water	¼ teaspoon brown sugar
½ teaspoon vinegar	

In a small bowl combine mustard with half the water. Stir to a smooth paste. Stir in vinegar, salt, sugar, and finally, in a thin stream, the remaining water. Store in refrigerator.

Makes about ¼ cup.

A SIMPLE CURRY POWDER

½ cup ground coriander   ¼ cup ground turmeric
¼ cup ground cumin   ¼ cup ground ginger

Mix well and bottle tightly.

A LESS SIMPLE CURRY POWDER

¼ cup coriander seed   1 tablespoon mustard seed
2 tablespoons saffron   ½ tablespoon crushed red
  threads   pepper
1 tablespoon cumin seed   1 tablespoon poppy seed

Grind together in a pepper mill, mix well, and bottle tightly.

3. Sizzling Snacks and Appetizers

THE FAR EAST offers some really choice appetizer recipes—sizzling textured tidbits that are a great relief from the slabs of Cheddar and globs of dip we are confronted with at parties. In the Orient, where all or most courses are set on the table at once, these little snacks are served at various points throughout a party dinner to pick up the appetite with contrasts in texture and flavor. They fit handily into our Western way of life as snacks to serve with hot soups and cold drinks, or as a first course.

A great many recipes in this chapter call for deep-frying. (Should I call it "deep sautéing"?) The dishes are not slimming, but they taste better than any potato chip you ever met and they're a triumph of the Oriental talent for turning handy odds and ends into real taste treats.

Deep-frying is simple in a *wok*, since only 3 cups of oil create lots of frying surface as well as the 2-to-3-inch depth necessary. Lots of head room, too: In a *wok* the oil never froths over. But any deep heavy kettle will do for deep-frying. Supplement the 3 cups of oil called for in frying recipes with enough to bring the depth to 3 inches. Strain the oil after use, refrigerate, covered. It is good as long as it remains clear and the color is right. For deep-frying, I much prefer a light corn oil to peanut oil.

CANTONESE EGG ROLLS

Egg Rolls are popular, inexpensive, and easy to make, especially if you have handy the pastry wrappers sold by Chinese specialty shops. If you are a purist and make your own with the recipe in Chapter 2, it will take longer. Offer Egg Rolls as appetizers, snacks, a first course, or part of an Oriental meal. Freeze extras.

2 tablespoons vegetable oil
2 cups shredded raw
   cabbage
1 large stalk celery, minced
1 cup shredded, cooked
   pork
1 cup raw shrimp, shelled,
   deveined, chopped
2 scallions, minced, or 1
   tablespoon minced onion

1½ teaspoons salt
⅛ teaspoon freshly grated
   black pepper
2½ teaspoons sugar
8 to 10 Egg-Roll Wrappers
1 egg, slightly beaten
3 cups oil
Chinese Mustard
Sweet-and-Sour Sauce

1. Prepare and measure the ingredients. Set 2 tablespoons oil, the cabbage, and the celery by the stove.

2. Set *wok* over high heat for 30 seconds, swirl in 2 tablespoons oil, count to 20, add cabbage and celery and stir-fry together for 2 minutes. Turn off heat, remove *wok* to the counter. Add to the *wok* the pork, shrimp, scallions, salt, pepper, sugar, and toss well. Fill pastry wrappers, using ⅒th to ⅛th of the mixture for each one. Roll and seal, as illustrated, with egg. Place rolls on oiled wax paper and let rest 1 hour.

3. Place paper-lined serving dish in a 250° oven. Set *wok* over high heat for 30 seconds, add 3 cups oil, heat to 375° or until a day-old cube of bread browns (about 1 minute). Place ½ to ⅓ of the rolls in the oil at once, and cook 4 to 5 minutes, or until golden brown, turning often. Drain and keep

warm until ready to serve. Serve with Chinese Mustard and Sweet-and-Sour Sauce.

Serves 4 to 5 or more if served with several other dishes.

SIZZLED NOODLE SHREDS

Leftover thin egg-noodle shreds make crisp, delicious appetizers when deep-fried. Flavor them with garlic, shrimp, crab, green onions, curry, or any ground herb you favor. If you have lots of noodles handy, do 1 cup at a time and vary the flavors.

1 cup cooked thin
  noodles, cold
¼ cup raw shrimp, shelled,
  deveined
White of ½ egg

⅛ teaspoon ginger, ground
½ teaspoon salt
⅛ teaspoon pepper
3 cups oil

1. Measure noodles into a medium bowl. Place shrimp, fresh or frozen, in blender and mix at low speed ½ minute. Mix shrimp bits into egg white with ginger, salt, pepper, but do not beat, just mix. Toss with noodles without attempting to separate stuck-together clumps.

2. Set *wok* over high heat for 30 seconds, add oil, and heat to 375° or until a day-old cube of bread browns (about 1 minute). Add noodles and cook without stirring until edges begin to brown. Use a slotted spoon or fork to break mass into 4 or 5 clumps, turn, and brown on the other side. Drain over *wok*, then on paper. Taste, and salt if necessary. Noodle Shreds can be fried ahead and browned in very hot oil just before serving. They are best when very crisp.

Serves 2.

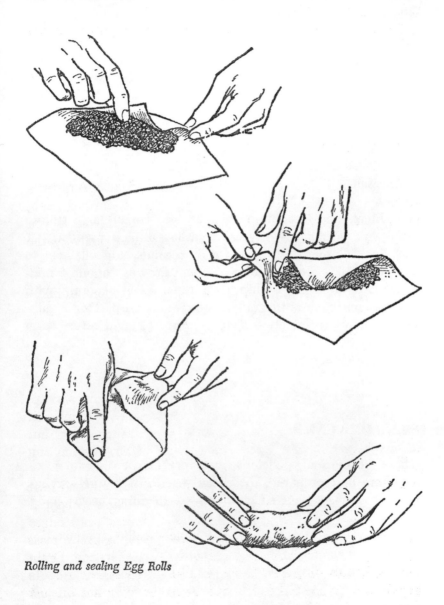

Rolling and sealing Egg Rolls

RICE CHIPS

This recipe should be called How-to-make-debits-into-credits —since it turns rice that has cooked dry and stuck to the bottom of the pot into appetizers. Flavor them with any herb you like.

Stuck-together cooked rice   Paprika
Garlic salt   3 cups oil

1. Break rice into lumpy shapes the size of large potato chips, and sprinkle lightly with garlic salt and paprika.
2. Set *wok* over high heat for 30 seconds, add oil, heat to 375° or until a day-old cube of bread browns (about 1 minute). Drop rice in, 1 chip at a time. Keep separate with spatula, and cook until golden brown and crisp, 1 or 2 minutes. Remove with slotted spoon, drain well, and serve warm or cold.
   1 cup rice serves 2 to 4.

SCALLION CAKES

These are unusual, delicious, and very inexpensive to make. They are best prepared ahead and fried just before serving. Not a fast snack, but so good it's worth doing occasionally.

½ cup water   1 bunch scallions, minced
1½ cups flour   fine
Sesame oil, or olive oil   2 cups fresh oil
    1 teaspoon salt

1. In a medium bowl mix water into flour until it forms a soft dough. Refrigerate 1 hour. This is important.

2. Flour a pastry board, turn out dough, and knead into a long roll about 1½ inches in diameter. Cut into quarters, cut each quarter into 5 pieces. Flour the board again and roll each piece into a thin pancake about 1½ inches in diameter. Brush pancakes with sesame oil, just a little, and sprinkle with minced scallion. Fold pancake in half, fold again in half, and roll between your palms into a ball. Now roll this ball flat again, making it the thinnest pancake you ever saw. Set on floured cookie sheet by the stove until ready to cook. Keep the cakes separate—if piled one on another, they may stick together.

3. Set *wok* over high heat 30 seconds, add oil and heat to 375° or until a day-old cube of bread browns (about 1 minute). If oil smokes, lower heat. Lift pancakes, one at a time, and float on hot oil until browned on underside. Flip (I use ice tongs), and brown other side. Drain over *wok* and on paper, add a little salt if you like, and serve at once. Do not refrigerate.

Serves 6 to 10.

SHRIMP CHIPS

Substitute 1 cup shelled, deveined shrimp, ground fine in blender, ½ teaspoon ground ginger, and 1 tablespoon soy sauce for scallions in the preceding Scallion Cakes recipe.

SHRIMP TOAST

This is a crisp, shrimp-flavored little appetizer that can be made at the last minute, or hours ahead and reheated in a medium oven. Leftovers freeze well, and can be crisped by refrying.

1 cup raw shrimp, shelled, deveined

4 water chestnuts, rinsed, minced

1 egg, slightly beaten

1 tablespoon dry sherry

¼ teaspoon ground ginger

½ teaspoon salt

¼ teaspoon black pepper

10 slices home-style bread

3 cups oil

1. Mince shrimp in blender at low speed, then mix in a medium bowl with water chestnuts, egg, sherry, ginger, salt, pepper. Remove crusts from bread, cut into even triangles (or shape with a cookie cutter) and spread firmly with shrimp paste. Make sure the paste is really stuck to bread edges so it won't separate. Refrigerate or freeze until ready to serve.

2. Place paper-lined serving dish in the oven at 250°, and have a Chinese sieve or a slotted spoon close to the stove. Set *wok* over high heat for 30 seconds, add oil, and heat to 350° or until a bit of bread sizzles *when it hits* the oil. Lower 3 or 4 slices of shrimp bread into the oil, shrimp side down. When edges brown, flip and brown on other side. Remove with slotted spoon and keep warm until ready to serve.

Serves 5 or 6.

SHRIMP BALLS, CHINA

Delicious, meaty little appetizers to serve with mustard and Sweet-and-Sour Sauce.

2 cups raw shrimp, shelled, deveined

1 egg, slightly beaten

1 tablespoon dry sherry

1 tablespoon soy sauce

1 teaspoon salt

2 teaspoons sugar

1 tablespoon cornstarch

1 cup lean ground pork (½ pound)

2 scallions, minced

3 cups oil

1. Roughly combine the shrimp, egg, sherry, soy sauce, salt, sugar, and cornstarch. Divide into two lots and mix each lot in blender at low speed. Mix the batches, and beat in ground pork and scallions. Refrigerate until ready to use.

2. Line a serving dish with paper and place in oven at 250°. Have handy a Chinese sieve or a slotted spoon. Set *wok* over high heat for 30 seconds, add oil, and heat to 350° or until a drop of batter sizzles and rises. Scoop shrimp mixture by rounded teaspoonfuls into oil, and cook to golden brown, 3 to 4 minutes. Remove with sieve, drain in oven. Serve hot on toothpicks and offer mustard or Sweet-and-Sour Sauce.

Serves 6 to 8.

SHRIMP BALLS, INDIA

Procedure is the same as for Shrimp Balls, China, but the ingredients are suited to curry-flavored meals.

2 cups raw shrimp, shelled, deveined
1 teaspoon ground turmeric
Pinch cayenne
½ teaspoon garlic powder
1 medium onion, minced

1 tablespoon cornstarch
1 teaspoon grated coconut
2 teaspoons bread crumbs
Salt to taste
3 cups oil

1. Combine shrimp, turmeric, cayenne, garlic powder, onion, and cornstarch. Blender-mix at low speed. Mix in coconut, bread crumbs, and salt. Refrigerate until ready to use.

2. Line a serving dish with paper and place in oven at 250°. Have handy a Chinese sieve or a slotted spoon. Set *wok* over high heat for 30 seconds, add oil, and heat to 350° or until a drop of batter sizzles and rises. Scoop shrimp mixture by rounded teaspoonfuls into oil, and cook to golden brown, 3 to 4 minutes. Remove with sieve, drain in oven. Serve hot on toothpicks, and offer mustard.

Serves 6.

SHRIMP TEMPURA

Batter-dipped shrimp, fried golden brown and served with Tempura Sauce, grated icicle radish, or minced scallions. Similar to the Chinese Phoenix-tailed Shrimp, this is a Japanese specialty. Clams and scallops, wiped dry, and lobster tails, shelled, cut into 1-inch pieces across the grain, can be substituted for the shrimp.

1 cup flour
1 teaspoon salt
½ teaspoon paprika
1 cup water less 2
  tablespoons
1 tablespoon oil
½ tablespoon dry sherry
1 tablespoon baking
  powder (optional)

1 pound raw shrimp,
  shelled, deveined
2 tablespoons soy sauce
1 teaspoon salt
2 teaspoons sugar
2 tablespoons ketchup
1 tablespoon horseradish
1 tablespoon lemon juice
3 cups oil

1. Place flour in a medium bowl, and stir with salt and paprika. Add water, mixing into flour with your fingers (it is easier). Stir in oil and sherry. If you like a puffy batter (I find it absorbs more grease), just before dipping shrimp add 1 tablespoon baking powder. If shrimp is fresh, leave on tails when you shell and devein. If frozen, thaw and wipe dry. Place batter and shrimp by stove with Chinese sieve or a slotted spoon.

2. In a small serving bowl, mix soy sauce, salt, and sugar. In another small bowl, mix ketchup, horseradish, lemon juice. Set aside to serve with the shrimp: the first is an Oriental sauce for Shrimp Tempura. The second is a Western sauce for Shrimp Tempura.

3. Place serving dish lined with paper in oven at 250°. Set *wok* over high heat for 30 seconds, add oil, heat to 350° or

until a drop of batter sizzles and rises. Dip shrimp into batter by the tail, coat well, fry a quarter at a time until golden brown, 3 to 4 minutes. Remove with sieve, drain, and keep hot. Serves 4 to 6.

JAPANESE EGG ROLLS

A kind of rolled-up egg pancake, with a surprising flavor. Any boneless white fish is suitable to use; sometimes I use fillets of small fish the children catch. These rolls have to cool for an hour, so you can make them well ahead of serving time.

6 eggs
½ teaspoon salt
3 tablespoons sugar
½ cup (4 ounces) flounder
4 tablespoons water

2 tablespoons Japanese soy sauce
3 tablespoons dry sherry
Vegetable oil

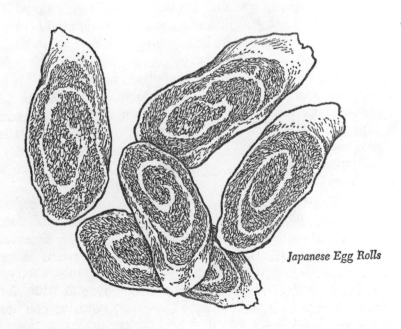

Japanese Egg Rolls

1. Break eggs into blender or mixer. Add salt, sugar, fish cut into 1-inch pieces, water, soy sauce, sherry, and blend on low for 1 minute.

2. Set *wok* over medium heat for 30 seconds, swirl in a few drops of oil, count to 5, pour in 2 or 3 tablespoons batter. Hold the handles of the *wok* with potholders and swirl batter around to make a thin pancake. When underside is a little brown, 1 or 2 minutes, roll up pancake and remove to serving platter. Repeat till batter is gone. Cool pancakes 1 hour, cut into halves or quarters, and serve.

Serves 8 to 10.

FRIED WON-TONS

These make better cocktail party appetizers than do Egg Rolls, and they're just as good and just as easy. Use Won-Ton Wrappers sold by Chinese specialty stores, or make your own with the recipe in Chapter 2. Freeze extras, but handle with care when frozen as they are quite brittle. Defrost before separating.

2 tablespoons vegetable oil
1 cup (½ pound) lean
   ground pork raw
2 cups shrimp, shelled,
   deveined, minced
2 tablespoons soy sauce
1 tablespoon dry sherry
1 teaspoon salt
6 water chestnuts, drained,
   minced

1 scallion, minced, or 1
   teaspoon minced onion
1 teaspoon cornstarch
2 tablespoons water
4 or 5 dozen Won-Ton
   Wrappers
1 egg, slightly beaten
3 cups oil
Sweet-and-Sour Sauce
Mustard

1. Prepare and measure oil, pork, shrimp, soy sauce, sherry, salt, water chestnuts, scallion. Mix cornstarch with water.

2. Set *wok* over high heat for 30 seconds, swirl in 2 tablespoons oil, count to 20, add pork and stir-fry until meat loses

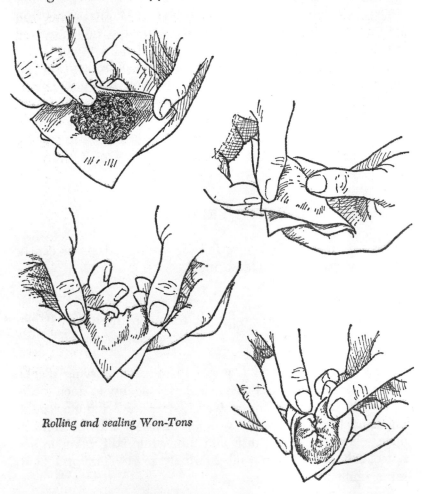

Rolling and sealing Won-Tons

pink, about 2 minutes. Add shrimp, soy sauce, wine, salt, water chestnuts, scallions, and stir-fry till shrimp turns pink, 2 to 3 minutes. Add cornstarch mixture, stir until ingredients thicken, then dish into a medium bowl and cool.

3. Place 1 teaspoon, more or less, of filling, in the center of each Won-Ton Wrapper, and roll and seal with egg as illustrated. Set on oiled wax paper until you are ready to cook. Freeze extras.

4. Heat oven to 250°. Place in it a serving dish lined with

paper. Have handy a Chinese sieve or a slotted spoon. Set *wok* over high heat for 30 seconds, add oil, heat to 375° or until a day-old cube of bread browns (about 1 minute). Fry Won-Tons 8 to 10 at a time until golden brown, about 2 minutes. Drain in oven at 250° while you finish the batch. Serve hot with Sweet-and-Sour Sauce and mustard, preferably Chinese.

Serves 10 to 12.

CRISPED MARINATED CELERY

Salad-like, this makes a nice foil for hot appetizers or can be served as part of a Chinese meal.

6 stalks white celery	½ teaspoon sugar
1 teaspoon soy sauce	1 teaspoon dry sherry
½ teaspoon salt	1 teaspoon sesame oil

Remove celery leaves (reserve to decorate serving plate), and cut stalks into sections 2 inches long by ½ inch wide. Blanch in rapidly boiling water to cover for 1 minute, counting from the moment the water returns to a boil. Drain at once. Place in serving dish and mix while still warm in soy sauce, salt, sugar, sherry, oil. Marinate in refrigerator 1 hour, serve chilled.

Serves 6.

SPICE SAUCE WITH FISH CHUNKS, SIAM

Batter-dipped fish chunks fried golden brown and served with a spicy hot sauce. Serve as appetizer, a first course, or the crispy fish part of a Chinese-style meal. Or, with rice, as dinner for two.

1 package (1 pound) frozen haddock or flounder
2 tablespoons white vinegar
½ teaspoon chili powder
½ cup Chicken Stock
2 tablespoons sugar
10 fresh mushrooms, minced
1 teaspoon ground ginger

3 scallions, minced
1 clove garlic, peeled, minced
2 tablespoons soy sauce
1 tablespoon cornstarch
1 cup flour
1 cup water
1 tablespoon olive oil
1 teaspoon salt
3 cups vegetable oil

1. Cut partially thawed fish into chunks 1 inch by ½ inch, and thaw. Wipe dry.

2. In a small saucepan put the vinegar with the chili powder, Chicken Stock, sugar, mushrooms, ginger, scallions, garlic, soy sauce. Stir in cornstarch and simmer over low heat, stirring constantly until sauce thickens, about 5 minutes. Add water if it becomes too thick.

3. Mix flour, water, olive oil, and salt into a lumpy batter. Since flours vary in their ability to absorb water, it may be necessary to add ⅛ cup flour to the batter to make it the right consistency. Test-fry a fish chunk and add flour if you prefer a thicker coat of batter.

4. Place serving dish lined with paper in oven at 250°. Have handy a Chinese sieve or a slotted spoon. Set *wok* over high heat for 30 seconds, add vegetable oil, heat to 350° or until a bit of batter sizzles and rises when it hits the oil. Dip fish chunks to coat with batter, drop one at a time into oil. Add only as many as *wok* holds comfortably. Fry to golden brown, about 3 to 4 minutes. Remove with slotted spoon, drain in oven. Serve hot with sauce.

Serves 6 as an appetizer.

TEA EGGS

Eggs hard-boiled in tea and flavorings, in a way that patterns the white, are a very decorative item for an appetizer tray. Chinese.

8 eggs
Water to cover
3 tablespoons black or dark tea
2 teaspoons salt
1 teaspoon red pepper
5 cloves star anise, or 1 teaspoon aniseed
2 teaspoons soy sauce

1. Place eggs in cold water to cover in a small saucepan. Set over medium heat, bring to a boil and simmer 10 minutes. Remove eggs from the saucepan, leaving water. Cool under running water, then crack shells *lightly* with a spoon so that they have a loose but *unbroken* shell.
2. To the water in the saucepan, add the tea, salt, pepper, anise, and soy sauce. Simmer eggs another 20 minutes. Remove shells, quarter eggs, and serve cold.
Serves 8.

STUFFED MUSHROOM CAPS

These are wet-steamed. If you do not have steam baskets for your *wok*, improvise by setting a platter on two oven-proof custard cups inside a roasting pan that has a lid. The flavor is more interesting if you use dried Chinese mushrooms, but excellent with fresh mushrooms, too.

1 cup (8-ounce can) crabmeat
14 to 18 dried Chinese mushroom caps, or large fresh mushroom caps
1 unbeaten egg white
1 teaspoon cornstarch
½ teaspoon ground ginger
1 teaspoon sherry
1 teaspoon salt

1. Drain and shred crabmeat and place in a medium bowl. Cover dried mushrooms (but not fresh) with boiling water and soak 20 minutes. Drain, squeeze dry. Stir egg white into crabmeat, then mix in cornstarch, ginger, sherry, and salt.

2. Arrange mushroom caps on steam-basket floor, or on a plate for an improvised steamer. Heap caps with crab filling. Pour boiling water into the *wok*, or improvised steamer, place steam basket over water, cover, steam—10 minutes for dry Chinese mushrooms, 20 minutes, or until caps begin to shrivel, for fresh mushrooms.

Serves 4 to 6, or more.

MEAT BALLS

Walnut-sized appetizers, pungent with garlic. Serve on toothpicks with a side bowl of Sweet-and-Sour Sauce. Save half, uncooked, for the freezer so you'll be able to make Sweet-and-Sour Meat Balls, page 98, a dinner dish.

12 dried Chinese mushrooms (optional)
1 pound lean ground pork
1 cup (8 ounces) water chestnuts, minced, or celery
½ cup (8-ounce can) crabmeat
1 teaspoon salt
2 teaspoons sugar
⅛ teaspoon black pepper
2 tablespoons minced onion
2 cloves garlic, peeled and crushed
¼ cup mushroom water
2 tablespoons soy sauce
Cornstarch
2 eggs
1 tablespoon water
3 cups oil
Sweet-and-Sour Sauce

1. Cover mushrooms with boiling water and soak 20 minutes. Measure pork into a large mixing bowl. Add drained, rinsed, minced water chestnuts, and drained, shredded crabmeat. Drain mushrooms, reserving water, mince mushrooms and

add to pork. Toss ingredients with salt, sugar, pepper, onion, garlic, ¼ cup mushroom water, and soy sauce. Roll into walnut-sized balls between your palms; half fill a small bowl with cornstarch, and roll each ball around in the bowl until well coated. Freeze a portion for another time, and refrigerate balance until serving time.

2. Place thawed or fresh Meat Balls by the stove, with the eggs mixed with the water. Set *wok* over high heat 30 seconds, add oil, heat to 350° or until a bit of bread sizzles when dropped into it. Dip balls in egg and water mixture, and fry 8 to 10 at a time, about 3 minutes. Serve hot with Sweet-and-Sour Sauce.

Serves 8 or more.

PAKORAS

This is a blessing when unexpected guests arrive and you've nothing to offer as appetizers. Main ingredient is most any juicy vegetable, including potatoes and even spinach. An Indian dish.

2⅛ cups buttermilk pancake
    mix
1 tablespoon oil
1 cup milk
1 tablespoon curry powder
1 teaspoon salt

Vegetable pieces (24 to 36)
    or sweet onion rings, ½
    inch thick
2 tablespoons flour
3 cups oil

1. In a large bowl blend pancake mix, oil, milk, curry powder, and salt. Peel vegetables, wipe dry, toss in 2 tablespoons flour.

2. Place serving dish, paper-lined, in oven at 250°. Have handy a Chinese sieve or a slotted spoon. Set *wok* over high heat for 30 seconds, add oil, and heat to 375° or until a day-old cube of bread browns (about 1 minute). Add vegetable

pieces to the batter, mix to coat well, and place one at a time on oil. Make sure there is room for each piece to float freely as it cooks. Fry golden brown, 3 to 4 minutes, remove with sieve, keep warm in oven until ready to serve.

Serves 6 to 8, or more.

PASTRY ROLLS, VIETNAM

These are called *Nems* in Vietnam; they are like a smaller Egg Roll. They can be made with quartered Egg-Roll Wrappers, but I prefer to do them in Won-Ton Wrappers, rolled as Egg Rolls. They are usually served with sauce made from fish sauce, and with lemon juice and chili powder, but I think they are nicer with mustard and Sweet-and-Sour Sauce. If you like *hot* foods, add a teaspoon of red pepper flakes instead of the pinch of chili powder. Freeze extras, uncooked, for another day.

12 dried Chinese
   mushrooms (optional)
1 egg, slightly beaten
1 tablespoon vegetable oil
1 tablespoon fish sauce or
   soy sauce
1 tablespoon lemon juice,
   strained
½ teaspoon salt
⅛ teaspoon black pepper
Pinch chili powder
1 small onion, minced
1 cup (½ pound) ground
   pork

1 cup cooked vermicelli,
   minced, or cooked rice
1 clove garlic, peeled,
   minced
2 cups raw shrimp, shelled,
   deveined, minced
1 cup bean sprouts, rinsed
15 Egg-Roll Wrappers,
   quartered, or 60 Won-Ton
   Wrappers
1 egg, slightly beaten
3 cups oil
Shredded lettuce
Sweet-and-Sour Sauce

1. Soak mushrooms in boiling water 20 minutes, drain, mince. Place in a medium bowl and mix with egg, 1 tablespoon oil,

fish sauce, lemon juice, salt, pepper, chili powder, onion, pork, vermicelli, garlic, shrimp, bean sprouts. Place 1 teaspoon of mixture on each wrapper, roll as illustrated (page 27), and seal with beaten egg. Set on oiled waxed paper until ready to cook. Freeze extras.

2. Set *wok* over high heat for 30 seconds, add oil, and heat to 350° or until a cube of bread sizzles. Fry a quarter at a time until golden brown, 2 or 3 minutes, drain, serve hot with shredded lettuce and Sweet-and-Sour Sauce.

Serves 10 or more.

EGGPLANT RELISH

This is more international than Oriental, but it blends well with groups of deep-fried appetizers, and is easy on the hostess since it keeps for days and can be made ahead.

1 medium eggplant
½ cup celery, minced
⅓ can pimiento strips, minced
1 clove garlic, peeled, minced
2 tablespoons capers, chopped

2 tablespoons minced parsley
1 sprig dill, snipped
¼ teaspoon oregano
½ teaspoon cumin, ground
¼ cup olive oil
¼ cup wine vinegar
½ teaspoon salt
⅛ teaspoon chili powder

Wash and stem eggplant, drop into boiling water to cover, and simmer 20 minutes, until tender but not mushy. Peel, chop into 1-inch cubes. Turn into large salad bowl with all other ingredients; mix well. Cover, refrigerate for a day, serve on crisped appetizers, raw celery or bland crackers.

Serves 12 or more.

BACON-WRAPPED WATER CHESTNUTS

Crisp and reminiscent of chestnuts in flavor, these appetizers aren't really Oriental in origin but fit well into Far Eastern meals. Prepare ahead, refrigerate, and roast at the last minute.

1 small can water chestnuts	8 to 10 strips bacon
2 tablespoons brown sugar	Toothpicks

1. Drain, rinse, dry chestnuts, count them, then mix well with brown sugar. Cut bacon into as many pieces as you have chestnuts, and be sure each piece is long enough to wrap completely around the chestnuts. Wrap chestnuts in bacon, and attach with toothpick. Refrigerate until ready to serve.

2. Heat oven to 450°. Roast chestnuts on foil until bacon is brown and crisp, about 15 minutes. Serve at once on paper napkins.

Serves 4 to 6.

4. Six Classic Soups

IN CHINA several soups are served during a gala meal. Thick soups appear early, broths late, and the latter replace tea, which is not offered at dinner in most areas. At family meals, one soup is set in the center of the table at the same time as the several other main dishes. Diners dip from the tureen with a small porcelain spoon.

The six classic soups here can be used either Eastern style or Western, except perhaps Mulligatawny, a thick Indian soup best for warming hungry skiers and filling teen-agers. Any of the others, served with Egg Rolls or a Fu Yung, make quickly prepared fancy luncheon fare.

Several of these soups are based on Chicken Stock (see Chapter 2). You can make this from scratch easily enough, and the Fast Chicken Stock, which is as handy as opening a can, is good enough to be a soup in itself. Simmer the Chicken or Beef Stock two minutes with paper-thin slices or small pieces of almost any vegetable—mushrooms, spinach, watercress—and you will have invented your own delicate Far Eastern soup.

WON-TON SOUP

Dumpling-like stuffed Won-Tons in chicken soup. With 10 Won-Tons per serving, it makes a complete meal. Served with

4, as here, it can begin a Western-style meal or accompany an Oriental-style dinner. Buy readymade Won-Ton Wrappers from one of the shops listed at the back of the book, or make your own using the recipe in Chapter 2. Uncooked leftover stuffed Won-Tons freeze well.

½ pound fresh spinach, washed, or 10-ounce package, frozen

4 cups (½ pound) lean pork, cooked

1½ tablespoons soy sauce

½ teaspoon fresh ginger, or ¼ teaspoon ground

1 teaspoon salt

5 dozen Won-Ton Wrappers, or 14 Egg-Roll Wrappers quartered

1 egg, slightly beaten

2 quarts boiling water

6 cups Chicken Stock, or canned chicken consommé

12 fresh spinach leaves (optional)

1. Cook spinach, drain, chop, and place in mixing bowl. Mince pork in blender, a third at a time, and add to spinach, with soy sauce, ginger, minced, and salt. Mix well.

2. Place about 1 teaspoon spinach filling in each Won-Ton Wrapper, roll and seal with egg as illustrated. Refrigerate or freeze until ready to use. Do not heap together, as they may stick. Handle frozen Won-Tons carefully; they are brittle until thawed.

3. Drop Won-Tons into 2 quarts boiling water over high heat. Return to a boil, reduce heat, simmer uncovered 5 minutes. Drain well.

4. Bring Chicken Stock to a boil over high heat, add Won-Tons, then spinach leaves, return to a boil, turn off heat and serve at once, placing 2 spinach leaves and 4 or 10 Won-Tons in each plate. Greens should be just wilted but still bright green.

Serves 6 or more.

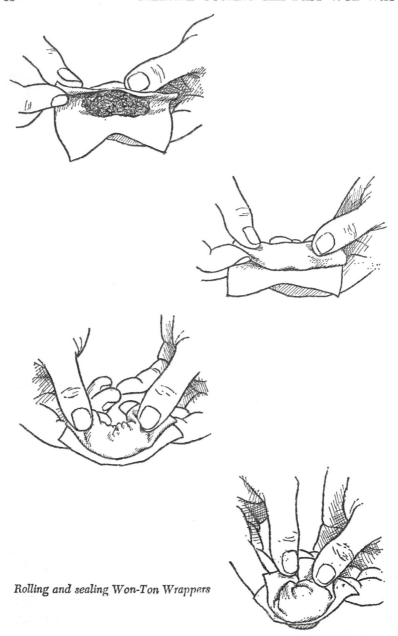

Rolling and sealing Won-Ton Wrappers

SOUR-AND-HOT SOUP

This is a classic of restaurant dinner menus, distinctly Chinese in character. The ingredients are available from specialty shops listed at the end of this book, and will keep indefinitely in airtight containers.

¼ cup dried tree fungus
¼ cup dried tiger lilies
¼ cup dried Chinese
   mushrooms
1 cake bean curd
   (optional)
3 cups Beef Stock, or
   canned beef consommé

2 tablespoons cornstarch
½ cup cold Beef Stock
1 tablespoon soy sauce
½ teaspoon black pepper
1½ tablespoons vinegar
1 egg
1 teaspoon water

Dried tiger lilies

1. Cover tree fungus, lilies, mushrooms with boiling water and soak 20 minutes. Drain, squeeze dry. Sliver mushrooms and bean curd, and add with fungus and lilies to Beef Stock. Place over medium heat, bring to a boil, and simmer 10 minutes. Stir in cornstarch mixed with cold Beef Stock, stir until soup thickens and clears. Add soy sauce, pepper, vinegar. Set aside until ready to serve.

2. Reheat soup to a simmer. Mix egg slightly with water in a small pitcher, and pour into simmering soup in a slow thin stream. Serve immediately.

Serves 4 to 6.

EGG DROP SOUP

Light, delicate Egg Drop Soup can be prepared in a scant minute or two, and with Egg Rolls makes a different and delightful luncheon. Fry the Egg Rolls just before you add the egg to the soup.

4 to 5 cups Chicken Stock, or canned chicken consommé
1 tablespoon cornstarch
½ teaspoon soy sauce
8 tablespoons Chicken Stock, cold

½ teaspoon salt
2 eggs
1 scallion, minced
1 teaspoon Chinese parsley, minced (optional)

1. Heat Chicken Stock to a simmer; mix cornstarch and soy sauce into 3 tablespoons cold Chicken Stock, add salt, pour into simmering soup, and stir until thick and clear. Set aside until ready to serve, then reheat to a simmer.

2. Break eggs into a small pitcher, mix very slightly, and pour in a thin, slow stream into soup. Turn off heat, stir once. Divide scallion and parsley among soup plates, and ladle in the soup. Serve at once.

Serves 4 to 6, more if part of a Chinese meal.

BIRD'S NEST SOUP

The nests, sold whole or broken in specialty shops, are gelatinous material produced by swifts living in South Sea islands. Bird's Nest Soup is a Chinese banquet item, not everyday fare. Soak the nest for 3 hours or overnight, pick out feathers with a tweezer, then rinse the nests clean in cold water.

5 cups of Chicken Stock, or canned chicken consommé
4 to 6 bird's nests, soaked, cleaned
1 teaspoon salt

1 teaspoon cooked ham, minced
4 tablespoons cooked chicken breast
1 tablespoon soy sauce
1 tablespoon sesame oil, or Chinese parsley, minced

Heat the stock to a simmer, add the prepared nests and salt, simmer uncovered for 20 minutes. Add ham, chicken, and soy sauce. Simmer 1 minute more, and serve at once with a drop or two of sesame oil or a pinch of minced Chinese parsley on each plate.

Serves 4 to 6.

VEGETABLE SOUP, JAPAN

A light, fast soup nice with Chinese meals, too.

2 teaspoons oil
1/4 cup dried Chinese mushrooms, or 1/2 cup fresh
1 cup (1/2 pound) lean pork
6 cups Chicken Stock, or canned chicken consommé
1 medium carrot

1/4 cup bamboo shoots, or 1 medium celery stalk
1 tablespoon soy sauce
1 cup chopped spinach, fresh or frozen and thawed
1/4 teaspoon ground ginger

1. Measure oil. Cover mushrooms with boiling water, soak 20 minutes, drain, and shred. Cut pork against the grain into shreds about 1 inch long and as thin as you can make them. If pork is lightly frozen, thinner shreds are possible. Measure stock. Cut carrot and bamboo shoots or celery into slivers 1 inch long and as thin as possible. Measure soy sauce, prepare spinach, measure ginger. Assemble all ingredients by the stove, in the order listed.

2. Set *wok* over medium heat for 30 seconds, swirl in oil, count to 10, add mushrooms and pork, stir-fry 5 minutes. Add stock, bring to a boil, and add carrot, bamboo shoots, and soy sauce, and simmer uncovered 5 minutes more. Add spinach and ginger, stir until spinach wilts, and serve at once, while spinach is still bright green.

Serves 6 to 8.

MULLIGATAWNY, INDIA

This is suited to any East Indian meal, and just great with hot rolls as a cold-weather snack.

½ cup dried lentils
7 cups water
2 tablespoons butter
1 small onion, chopped
1 clove garlic, peeled, minced
1 teaspoon ground coriander

½ teaspoon ground cumin
⅛ teaspoon red pepper flakes (more if you like)
2 teaspoons turmeric or curry
1 teaspoon lime or lemon juice, strained
1 teaspoon salt

1. Wash and drain lentils, bring to a boil with the water in a heavy soup kettle. Simmer covered until lentils are soft, 1 hour or more. Stir occasionally; lentils tend to stick and burn.

2. Melt butter in a small saucepan over medium heat. Add onion, garlic, coriander, cumin, pepper, turmeric. Simmer until onion is golden, about 5 minutes. Stir into cooked lentils, and add a little water if soup has become too thick. Add lemon juice and salt, and simmer 15 minutes more. Serve hot.

Serves 4 to 6.

5. Minute Eggs
and the Fu Yungs

EGGS FU YUNG (or Foo Young) and Thousand-Year-Old Eggs (or Hundred-Year Old Eggs; are probably the two best-known Oriental egg dishes. Thousand-Year Eggs, I am sorry to report, are limed and aged only one hundred days, not buried for centuries. They are reminiscent of hard-boiled eggs, but gray-green-brown in color once the mud is washed off and the shell removed. They are served quartered as an appetizer with a little soy sauce. The specialty shops carry them.

In the East, eggs are fried and served with soy sauce, dropped (Egg Drop Soup), hard-boiled (Tea Eggs), and stirred. "Stirred" means beaten, poured into hot oil, with cooked portions pushed to one side until the whole is set. Fu Yungs are more glamorous. They are delicate, frothy, fried concoctions of meat or seafood and vegetables, mixed with unbeaten egg.

The Fu Yungs, and most of the egg recipes, are handy when your cupboard is bare; they make an egg into a beautiful experience. Serve them with soup for luncheon or as an extra dish at an Oriental dinner.

FU YUNG WITH SHRIMP OR LOBSTER

It sounds like an omelet, but it is deliciously different. A quick easy extra dish for a full-scale Chinese dinner—or with soup a delightful luncheon.

1 cup (8 ounces) raw shrimp, or lobster	4 scallions, or 1 small onion, shredded
1 medium celery stalk	¼ teaspoon ground ginger
½ cup chopped mushrooms	5 large eggs, *not beaten*
1 cup shredded iceberg lettuce, or bean sprouts	1 cup fresh oil

1. Use fresh or thawed raw shrimp or lobster, shelled. Devein shrimp, chop coarsely. Chop celery into rounds ⅛ inch thick. Place in large mixing bowl with mushrooms, lettuce, scallions, and toss well with ginger. Break eggs over mixture, and combine gently. Do not beat eggs.

2. Place napkin-lined serving platter in oven at 250°. Have handy shrimp mixture, oil, a Chinese sieve or slotted spoon. Set *wok* over high heat for 30 seconds, swirl in oil, heat 1 minute. Gently float ¼ of the shrimp mixture on oil. Don't scramble or mix in any way. When edges turn brown, about 1 minute, use sieve and a spoon to flip cake onto its other side. When brown, lift gently with sieve, drain well over oil, and keep warm in oven while you cook remaining three portions.

Serves 4.

FU YUNG WITH CRAB

Substitute 1 cup shredded crabmeat, raw or cooked, tossed with 1 tablespoon dry sherry, use bean sprouts if possible, and omit scallions. Follow preceding recipe for Fu Yung with Shrimp.

FU YUNG WITH ROAST PORK

Substitute 1 cup leftover pork, 3 stalks celery, 2 scallions, soy sauce, for corresponding ingredients in Fu Yung with Shrimp. Omit ginger.

1 cup roasted pork,
  shredded
3 stalks celery
2 scallions
1 cup shredded lettuce, or
  bean sprouts

½ cup chopped mushrooms
2 tablespoons soy sauce
2 teaspoons sugar
5 large eggs, not beaten
1 cup fresh oil

1. Measure the shredded pork. Shred celery, scallions, and lettuce in large mixing bowl with mushrooms, and toss well with soy sauce and sugar. Break eggs over mixture and combine gently.

2. Place napkin-lined serving platter in oven at 250°. Have handy pork mixture, oil, a Chinese sieve or slotted spoon. Set *wok* over high heat for 30 seconds, swirl in oil, heat 1 minute. Gently float ¼ of the pork mixture on oil. Don't scramble or mix in any way. When edges turn brown, about 1 minute, use sieve and a spoon to flip cake onto other side. When brown, lift gently with sieve, drain well over oil, and keep warm in oven while you cook remaining three portions.

Serves 4.

LOBSTER OMELET

I use frozen South African lobster tails, unless we have available fresh lobster meat at a reasonable price. A nice luncheon dish.

1 tablespoon oil	¼ cup shredded onion
8 ounces raw lobster tails, shelled	3 tablespoons oil
	6 eggs, slightly beaten
2 tablespoons soy sauce	½ cup water
¼ teaspoon ground ginger	1 teaspoon salt
¼ cup bean sprouts, or minced celery	

1. Measure oil. Cut lobsters across the grain into pieces ½ inch thick. Measure soy sauce, ginger. Rinse sprouts and drain well. Measure onion, and oil, and mix eggs slightly with water and salt. Place all ingredients by the stove in the order listed. Have handy 2 potholders and a pad of paper towels.

2. Set *wok* over medium-high heat for 30 seconds, swirl in 1 tablespoon oil, count to 10, add lobster pieces, stir-fry 1 minute. Add soy sauce, stir twice. Add ginger, sprouts, onion, and stir-fry 3 minutes. Remove to serving dish. Use paper towel to wipe out *wok*.

3. Reheat *wok*, swirl in 3 tablespoons oil, count to 30, pour in egg mixture. Use potholders to grasp *wok* handles, lift *wok* and swirl egg up around sides so it can all cook. Just before it has set, spread lobster over the center of the omelet. Fold right and left edges across the center, so that they overlap. Cook 2 minutes more. Flip omelet, cook 1 minute more.

Serves 4, more if other dishes are offered.

OMELET, INDIA

Stuffed with onions and tomato, flavored with coriander and saffron—very nice with Indian foods.

6 eggs, slightly beaten
5 tablespoons butter
3 medium onions
2 medium tomatoes
2 teaspoons coriander, ground
1 teaspoon saffron

¼ teaspoon black pepper
Salt to taste
½ cup beef consommé, or water
2 tablespoons yogurt
1½ tablespoons lemon juice

1. Blend eggs briefly. Measure butter. Peel onions, slice into rounds ¼ inch thick, and place with tomatoes, quartered, in a small saucepan with coriander, saffron, pepper, salt, and beef consommé. Simmer over medium heat 10 minutes. Strain, reserving liquid. Place with yogurt, lemon juice, eggs, and butter by the stove.

2. Set *wok* over medium heat for 30 seconds. Melt butter, add eggs, spread and cook as an omelet, until half dry. Place cooked onion and tomato mixture over the center. Fold right and left edges inward to overlap. Simmer another few minutes. Remove and keep warm.

3. Turn heat to high, stir in yogurt, lemon juice, and cooking liquid from tomato mixture. Simmer about 6 minutes, until liquid reduces and thickens. Serve over omelet.

Serves 4 to 6.

CHICKEN CAKES, CANTON

Crisp little chicken cakes to serve as part of a larger meal. A nice way to dispose of chicken leftovers.

5 eggs	2 tablespoons flour
1 cup cooked diced chicken	½ cup minced mushrooms
2 teaspoons soy sauce	2 scallions, chopped or 1 tablespoon minced onion
¼ teaspoon black pepper	1 cup fresh oil
½ cup (4 ounces) water chestnuts	Salt to taste
	Chinese mustard

1. Break eggs into blender, turn on low, add chicken, soy sauce, pepper, water chestnuts, and flour. Pour into medium bowl, mix well with mushrooms and scallions. Set by the stove with the oil, a Chinese sieve or a slotted spoon. Place serving dish lined with paper towel in oven at 250°.

2. Set *wok* over high heat for 30 seconds, swirl in oil, heat to 350° or until a drop of batter sizzles. Add mixture 1 tablespoon at a time to the oil until *wok* is full. Flip cakes over as they brown on the underside, about 1 minute. Remove with sieve, drain in serving dish and keep warm. Serve with salt and mustard.

Serves 2 to 4, more if other dishes are offered.

FU YUNG, VIETNAM

One of several dishes set on the table simultaneously, as in a Chinese meal. Serve guests a rice bowl and a small side dish of sauce containing 2 tablespoons soy sauce, oyster sauce, or fish sauce, mixed with red pepper, lemon juice, and crushed garlic to taste.

4 tablespoons oil, or pork
fat
3 small onions, minced
¼ pound ground beef
1 cup (8 ounces) bean
sprouts

5 eggs, *lightly beaten*
Ground black pepper
2 teaspoons fish sauce or
oyster sauce or soy sauce

1. Set oil, onions, and beef by the stove. Rinse sprouts in cold water, drain, measure, and set by the stove with the eggs mixed lightly with pepper and fish sauce.

2. Set *wok* over medium heat for 30 seconds, swirl in oil, count to 30, add onions and stir-fry 1 minute. Add meat and stir-fry 1 minute. Add sprouts, stir-fry 3 minutes. Pour egg mixture over the ingredients in the *wok*. As portions cook, push them to the side so the remainder will fall into the center of the *wok* and cook. When underside is brown, flip and cook to light brown on the other side. Serve at once.

Serves 3 to 4, more if several dishes are offered.

MEAT TURNOVERS

Delicious little turnovers to serve with a full Chinese-style meal. Use ground beef if pork isn't available.

1½ cups (¾ pound) lean
ground pork
1 teaspoon sesame or olive
oil
1 scallion, minced
½ teaspoon soy sauce
¼ teaspoon sugar
½ teaspoon salt

1 tablespoon chicken fat, or
oil
4 eggs, slightly beaten
2 tablespoons water
1 tablespoon soy sauce
1 tablespoon chicken fat, or
oil
Sweet-and-Sour Sauce

1. Combine in a medium bowl the pork, sesame oil, scallion, soy sauce, sugar, and salt. Set *wok* over medium heat 30 seconds, stir in 1 tablespoon chicken fat, count to 30, add

pork mixture and stir-fry 2 minutes. Turn off heat. Return pork to mixing bowl. Mix eggs with water and soy sauce, and set by the stove with chicken fat. Place serving dish in oven at 250°. Have handy 2 potholders.

2. Turn heat under *wok* to medium high, and when *wok* begins to smoke a little, add a bit of chicken fat, swirl to coat sides. Pour about ⅛th of egg mixture into *wok*, lift *wok* and swirl egg to form 3-inch pancake. When it has dried, place ⅛th of meat filling in center, fold in half, press edges to seal, flip and cook while you count to 30. Keep warm until remaining 7 pancakes are done. Serve with Sweet-and-Sour Sauce or just with salt and pepper.

Serves 4, more if other dishes are offered.

EGGS WITH CABBAGE, VIETNAM

Delicious when you can get young, tender cabbage. Use only leafy portions, omit the hard core.

2 tablespoons oil	4 eggs
1 small fresh green cabbage	Juice 1 lemon
1 teaspoon oyster or fish sauce	⅛ teaspoon red pepper (or less)

1. Measure oil, shred cabbage, omitting core. Place with all other ingredients close to the stove in the order listed.

2. Set *wok* over medium-high heat for 30 seconds, swirl in the oil, count to 30, add cabbage shreds and stir-fry until bright green and wilting, about 5 minutes. Stir in oyster sauce, mix well, then add eggs, 1 at a time, mixing in gently to combine with cabbage shreds. When eggs are set, but before they become dry and hard, sprinkle with lemon juice, turn them over, sprinkle with pepper. Serve at once, and offer salt at the table.

Serves 2 to 4, more if several dishes are offered.

EGG CURRY, INDIA

Hard-boiled eggs, tomatoes, and mushrooms in a creamy sauce based on yogurt. Takes about 1 hour. Nice Sunday supper with plain boiled rice.

¼ cup oil
1 large onion, chopped
3 slices fresh ginger, minced, or 1 teaspoon ground ginger
2 tablespoons minced parsley
1 teaspoon turmeric
2 teaspoons curry powder

3 tomatoes, quartered
8 ounces plain yogurt
¼ pound mushrooms, chopped
6 hard-boiled eggs, shelled, halved
2 tablespoons strained lemon juice

1. Place the ingredients by the stove in the order listed.
2. Set *wok* over medium heat, stir in oil, count to 30, add onions and ginger, stir-fry until onions are golden, 3 to 4 minutes. Lower heat. Add parsley, turmeric, curry, and simmer uncovered 4 minutes, stirring occasionally. Add tomatoes, simmer 8 minutes. Add yogurt and mushrooms, mix well, simmer 15 minutes. Add egg halves, simmer 3 minutes. Just before you remove the dish, add lemon juice and stir 1 minute. Serve with salt.
Serves 4 to 6.

6. Rice and the Flavored Rices

WHAT PASTA is to Italy, bread to France, and the potato to Anglo-Saxon countries, rice is to the East. Some northern regions also rely on other grains, including wheat in the form of unleavened bread.

Rice is a cereal rich in iron, phosphorus, vitamins B_1 and G. Of the white, refined rices, converted rice retains the most nutrients, which is nice, since it also is the easiest to cook to perfection. Another school of Oriental dining (my husband included) prefers the short-grained rices, which are stickier and simpler to handle with chopsticks. (I never got the hang of chopsticks.) Glutinous varieties are really sticky and used mainly for desserts and the Chinese breakfast gruel, *congee*. Rinsed, rather than soaked, and started in boiling water, rice retains most of its nutritional content.

At a traditional Chinese dinner, a small bowl of plain un-salted boiled rice (and the wine) are the only foods served to individuals; all other dishes are set in the center of the table and eaten from directly by everyone. The flavorful fried rices (which are best when grainy and made from left-overs) are served as main dishes and shared. Sometimes I serve them in place of boiled rice, however. It is a serious breach of etiquette to leave even one grain of the boiled rice in the bowl.

In India, rice appears on each diner's tray in a small bowl, and may be plain boiled rice or a flavored *pulao,* which is raw rice first fried with flavorings, then simmered in water.

STICKY RICE FOR CHOPSTICKS

My husband, David, likes to eat with chopsticks, and he likes his rice this way:

2 cups oval rice   3½ cups water, cold

Wash rice in two changes of water. Place in 3- to 4-quart kettle with tightly fitting lid. Add water, place over high heat, bring to a boil, uncovered. Lower heat to minimum, cover tightly, simmer 20 minutes, or until all water is absorbed and rice is soft and fluffy. If it sticks to the bottom, scoop out all soft rice and serve, save crusty stuck-together rice to make Rice Chips (Chapter 3).

Serves 4 to 6.

GLUTINOUS RICE

This is available in specialty shops and is most often used to make desserts and in some areas of China a gruel-like breakfast food.

1½ cups glutinous rice   3 cups water, cold

Wash rice in two changes of water, place in 3- to 4-quart kettle with tightly fitting lid. Add water, place over high heat, bring to a boil uncovered. Lower heat to minimum, cover tightly, simmer 30 minutes until soft and dry. It will be sticky.

Makes about 4 cups.

POT-FRIED RICE, VIETNAM

Try this for family meals as a variation on the boiled-rice theme.

2 cups rice	2 teaspoons salt
2 tablespoons butter or	1 clove garlic, minced
pork or chicken drippings	1¾ cups boiling water

1. Wash rice in two changes of water, drain well. Melt butter in a heavy 3- to 4-quart kettle that has a tightly fitting lid. Add rice, salt, and garlic and stir-fry over medium heat about 10 minutes, until grains have golden tinge and opaque look.

2. Pour boiling water over the rice, turn heat to high, cover, cook 5 minutes. Lower heat. Remove lid and fluff rice. Cover, and cook over lowest heat for 15 to 20 minutes, until rice is just tender.

Serves 4 to 6.

VINEGARED RICE, JAPAN

This is called *sushi* and is eaten with cooked or raw fish such as tuna. See Sashimi, in Chapter 8.

2 cups rice	1 teaspoon sugar
1⅘ cups water	2 teaspoons salt
¼ cup vinegar	¼ teaspoon MSG

1. Three hours before mealtime, wash rice well. Light flame under 1⅘ cups of water in a large kettle with a tight-fitting lid, and *just before* water boils up, drop in the rice. Bring water to a boil, lower heat, cover, and simmer 10 minutes. Rice should be firm and rather hard.

2. Place rice in shallow bowl, cool quickly while stirring in vinegar mixed with sugar, salt, and MSG. When served with raw fish, each portion of rice is shaped into an oval, and a slice of raw fish is pressed upon it.

Serves 2 to 4.

SIZZLING RICE PATTIES

A crisp, mildly flavored cake to make with leftover rice. This recipe includes shrimp, but the rice cakes are almost as good plain, served topped with bits of leftover reheated Chinese dishes or Indian curry with sauce. To vary, substitute any seafood, or cooked pork. Make smaller patties when planned as part of a large meal.

Per person:

1 egg white	8 shrimp, fresh or frozen
1 teaspoon dry sherry	and thawed, shelled,
⅛ teaspoon ground ginger	deveined, chopped
½ teaspoon soy sauce	1 cup cooked rice
¼ teaspoon salt	3 cups oil
	Salt

1. Mix, *but do not beat,* egg white, sherry, ginger, soy sauce, salt, chopped shrimp. Add rice and stir until bound by egg white; you want the rice to stick together. Set by the stove with a Chinese sieve.

2. Set *wok* over high heat for 30 seconds, add oil, and heat to 350° or until a bit of bread sizzles quickly. Slide mixture for 1 rice patty onto oil, and cook without stirring for 3 minutes or until golden along edges. Use spatula and large spoon to turn without breaking, and cook 2 minutes on underside or until golden brown. Drain well, salt lightly. Can be kept warm briefly in 250° oven.

SAFFRON RICE, INDIA

This is *kedgeree* or *khichri,* an aromatic rice course that accompanies meat or vegetable curries. It is served with chutney.

1 teaspoon oil
2 sticks butter
2 large onions, sliced
¼ teaspoon ground ginger
⅛ teaspoon ground clove
⅛ teaspoon cinnamon
¼ teaspoon cardamom,
  ground

¼ teaspoon fenugreek,
  ground
2 cups raw rice
4 cups water
½ teaspoon saffron
2 tablespoons water

1. Set *wok* or heavy kettle with tightly fitting lid over medium heat. Coat with oil, add half the butter and melt. Add *half* the onions and stir-fry until golden, 3 to 5 minutes. Add ginger, clove, cinnamon, cardamom, fenugreek, and stir-fry 1 minute. Add rice, stir-fry 5 to 8 minutes, until it has opaque look. Add water, stir well, cover, simmer until water has been absorbed, about 15 minutes. Check to make sure rice isn't sticking.

2. While rice cooks, simmer remaining onions in remaining butter until golden. Add to rice with saffron soaked in 2 tablespoons water. Toss lightly, cook another 3 minutes, covered, and serve.

Serves 6 to 8.

RICE AND POTATOES, PAKISTAN

We serve this with strong East Indian meat curries, or with roasted pork or chicken.

1 stick butter
2 medium onions, minced
2 cups rice
4 medium potatoes, peeled,
  quartered
1 teaspoon salt
1 teaspoon turmeric or
  curry

1 teaspoon coriander,
  ground
2 cloves garlic, peeled,
  minced
1 teaspoon fresh ginger,
  minced, or ½ teaspoon
  ground
4½ cups boiling water

Melt butter over medium heat in a *wok* or a heavy large kettle with a tightly fitting lid. Add onions and stir-fry 10 minutes. Add rice, mix well. Add potatoes, salt, turmeric, coriander, garlic, ginger; mix again. Add water, return to a boil, reduce heat, cover, and simmer 30 minutes, or until potatoes are tender and rice is cooked. Check occasionally to make sure rice isn't sticking.

Serves 6 to 10.

FRIED RICE, CANTON

A strongly flavored, grainy-textured fried rice that goes well with many stir-fried meat and vegetable dishes. The dried shrimp are sold at Chinese specialty shops, and keep indefinitely; frozen raw shrimp can be substituted and create a more delicate flavor. Very good, and it can be prepared ahead and kept warm indefinitely.

2 heaping tablespoons
  bacon fat
½ cup dried shrimp, or 1
  cup raw shrimp, shelled,
  deveined
2 tablespoons seedless dark
  raisins
⅓ cup prosciutto or
  Smithfield ham or boiled
  ham

½ cup walnut meats,
  broken
½ cup slivered almonds
3 scallions, chopped
2 tablespoons soy sauce
½ teaspoon salt
¼ cup frozen peas, thawed
3–4 cups cooked rice, cold

1. Measure bacon fat; blender-chop the dried or frozen shrimp; soak raisins 5 minutes in boiling water, drain. Blender-chop prosciutto or ham. Measure walnuts and almonds. Chop scallions. Set these ingredients, with soy sauce, salt, peas, and cooked (preferably leftover day-old) rice, by the stove in the order listed.

2. Set *wok* over high heat 30 seconds, swirl in fat. When it has melted, add shrimp. Stir-fry 1 minute. Add raisins, toss. Add ham, toss. Add walnuts and almonds, toss. Add scallions, and stir-fry 1 minute. Add soy sauce, salt, and peas; mix well. Add cooked rice, mix thoroughly, and stir-fry 2 minutes more, or until rice has grainy texture and is hot. Keep warm in 250° oven until ready to serve.

Serves 4 to 6, more if other dishes are offered.

THREE-FLAVORS FRIED RICE

Shrimp, pork, and chicken flavor this fried rice. To make Chicken Fried Rice or Pork Fried Rice or Shrimp Fried Rice, use 3 cups of chicken, pork, or shrimp, instead of 1 cup of each; with shrimp, add ¼ teaspoon minced fresh ginger. An easy, one-dish meal for 6, and good patio fare.

¼ cup chicken fat, or roast pork fat, or oil
2 scallions, chopped
1 cup raw shrimp, shelled, deveined, diced
½ teaspoon salt
2 eggs, slightly beaten
1 cup cooked pork, diced

1 cup cooked chicken, diced
4 cups cooked rice, cold
¼ cup soy sauce (minus 1 tablespoon if imported soy sauce)
¼ teaspoon black pepper
⅛ teaspoon ground ginger
1 cup lettuce, shredded

1. Set ingredients, prepared and measured, by the stove in the order listed.

2. Set *wok* over high heat for 30 seconds, swirl in *half* the

fat, count to 20, add scallions, and brown lightly. Add shrimp, stir-fry 3 minutes. Salt. Add eggs, scramble until not quite cooked. Remove to a warm plate.

3. Swirl remaining fat into the *wok*, count to 20, add pork and chicken, and stir-fry 2 minutes. Add rice, soy sauce, pepper, and ginger; stir and toss until heated. Add scrambled eggs; stir and toss half a minute. Add lettuce; stir and toss until mixed. Serve at once, before lettuce softens.

Serves 6, more if other dishes are offered.

FRIED RICE WITH HAM, EGGS, AND PEAS

Pretty, mildly flavored with a bit of ham. Texture should be grainy.

3 tablespoons ham fat, or oil	½ cup frozen peas, thawed, or minced celery
2 eggs, slightly beaten	½ cup cooked ham, diced
3 cups cooked rice, cold	3 scallions, chopped
1 teaspoon salt	1 tablespoon dry sherry

1. Set ingredients, prepared and measured, by the stove in the order listed.

2. Set *wok* over high heat for 30 seconds, swirl in *1* tablespoon fat, count to 20, add eggs, reduce heat. As eggs set, push cooked portion to one side so remainder can reach heat. When all egg is set but before it browns or dries, transfer to a bowl and break into large shreds.

3. Turn heat to medium high, add remaining fat, count to 20, add rice, stir and toss until hot. Add salt, peas, ham, stir-fry 2 minutes. Add eggs, scallions, stir to mix. Add sherry, stir and toss until mixture is piping hot. Serve at once.

Serves 2 to 4, more if other dishes are offered.

7. Noodles and the Chow Meins

"MEIN" IS THAT unleavened wheat product we call noodles, and it takes the place of rice in areas of northern China. Perfectionists prefer theirs handmade and "swung," an intricate art, as far as I can make out, which produces round noodles instead of noodles that are flat. Fresh flat noodles are amazingly easy to make and quite good. However, commercial dried egg noodles are almost as good and lots, lots easier. I serve noodles instead of rice when I am in a tearing hurry, because they cook more quickly.

Chow Mein (*ch'ao mien* also) is made with leftover noodles, usually. In America Chow Mein refers to a hard, fried and dried little thing like a tasteless pretzel, but in China, Chow Mein means noodles freshly fried and served *under* a sauce. Lo Mein means noodles warmed *in* a sauce.

Transparent noodles are bean-thread or cellophane noodles. They are a delicacy made of mung beans and essential to only a few recipes, among them Sukiyaki. They're sold in 6-ounce and smaller packages in specialty shops and keep indefinitely.

HOMEMADE FRESH NOODLES

This is intended to be read rather than done, though you might like to try it once. Eggs should be large and fresh.

4 eggs   3 cups flour

1. Beat eggs lightly. Stir in flour, and make a soft dough. Cover with damp cloth and let stand at room temperature for 20 minutes to 1 hour.
2. Sprinkle flour on pastry board. Roll dough, keeping both sides well floured, until dough is as thin as commercial egg noodles. Fold dough into several thicknesses in the length, as you fold a business letter. Use a sharp knife to cut into strips the width of packaged egg noodles. Use fresh.
    Serves 8 or more.

PORK CHOW MEIN WITH SHRIMP

Cooked noodles reheated, topped with delicious and substantial sauce. A complete meal for 2 to 4, and very fast if cooked noodles are available. To vary, substitute cooked chicken, beef, or ham for pork.

4 tablespoons pork or chicken fat, or oil
1 pound (2 cups) boned raw pork, or cooked pork, shredded
1 cup raw shrimp, shelled, deveined, chopped
1 cup mushrooms
4 medium stalks celery, shredded

4 scallions, shredded, or 2 tablespoons onion, minced
4 tablespoons soy sauce
1 teaspoon salt
1 tablespoon cornstarch
1 cup Chicken Stock, or water
4 to 6 cups cooked medium noodles (about 8 ounces)

1. Measure fat and pork; prepare shrimp; wipe mushrooms and cut into lengths ⅛ inch thick; shred celery, scallions; measure soy sauce. Mix salt and cornstarch with Chicken Stock. Measure noodles. Place all ingredients by the stove in the order listed.

2. Set *wok* over high heat for 30 seconds, swirl in *half* the fat, count to 20, add pork shreds and shrimp, stir-fry 1 minute. (If pork is raw, stir-fry first 3 minutes, then add shrimp.) Add mushrooms, celery, scallions, soy sauce; stir-fry 3 minutes more. Pour cornstarch mixture down side of *wok*, stir until thick and clear. Check seasonings and add more soy or salt if necessary.

3. In a heavy-bottomed skillet, melt remaining fat, and re-heat cooked noodles. Place noodles in serving dish, pour contents of *wok* over them and serve piping hot. Can be kept warm until ready to serve.

Serves 4 to 6, more if other dishes are offered.

PORK CHOW MEIN WITH MUSHROOMS

Meatier in flavor than Chow Mein with Shrimp. Nice with stir-fried Italian beans, and a garlicky green salad, European-style. If you can, cook noodles the day before and press flat into pie plate before refrigerating; this makes a big noodle pancake which is browned before the pork and mushroom sauce is added.

4 tablespoons pork fat, or
   vegetable oil
2 cups cooked pork,
   shredded
1 clove garlic, peeled,
   smashed
1 medium onion, chopped
2 cups fresh mushrooms,
   chopped

1 can bean sprouts
4 tablespoons soy sauce
3 tablespoons cornstarch
2 cups Chicken Stock, or
   water
4 to 5 cups fine noodles,
   cooked
1 tablespoon chopped
   scallions

1. Measure fat and pork; prepare garlic, onion, mushrooms. Drain bean sprouts, rinse in cold water, drain again. Measure soy sauce; mix cornstarch with Chicken Stock. Place with all ingredients by the stove in the order listed.

2. Set *wok* over high heat for 30 seconds, swirl in *half* the fat, count to 10. Add pork; stir-fry until lightly browned. Add garlic and onion; mix. Add mushrooms; stir-fry 3 minutes. Add bean sprouts; stir-fry 1 minute. Add soy sauce and pour cornstarch mixture down side of *wok*. Stir until it thickens and clears.

3. In a large, heavy skillet, melt remaining fat over high heat. Turn cooked noodles into skillet, press flat, brown. Turn carefully with spatula and pancake turner, and brown other side. Set on large serving dish and pour contents of *wok* over noodle cake. Sprinkle with scallions; serve soy sauce at the table.

Serves 4 to 6, more if other dishes are offered.

CHICKEN LO MEIN

A delicately flavored one-dish dinner for two. Served with any seafood or fish, deep-fried, it will make dinner for 3 or 4.

2 tablespoons chicken fat, or oil	1 cup Chicken Stock, or water
2 cups cooked diced chicken	2 tablespoons soy sauce
½ cup celery cabbage, or cabbage	1½ tablespoons cornstarch
	2 tablespoons water
½ cup celery, shredded	Salt and pepper to taste
½ cup bean sprouts	4 to 5 cups (8 ounces) cooked fine noodles
1 teaspoon sugar	2 scallions, minced

1. Measure fat and chicken. Shred celery cabbage or grate domestic cabbage on coarse side of grater. Measure celery, sprouts, rinsed and drained, sugar, Chicken Stock. Mix soy

sauce and cornstarch with water. Place all ingredients by the stove in the order listed.

2. Set *wok* over high heat for 30 seconds, swirl in fat, count to 20, add chicken and stir-fry 1 minute. Add cabbage; toss. Add celery; toss. Add bean sprouts and sugar, and stir-fry 1 minute more. Pour Chicken Stock down side of *wok*, push all ingredients down into the Stock, cover *wok*, lower heat to medium, and simmer 10 minutes. Add cornstarch mixture; stir until sauce thickens and clears. Taste and correct seasonings. Stir in noodles; heat through. Serve sprinkled with scallions. Offer soy sauce at the table. Can be reheated.

Serves 2 to 4, more if other dishes are offered.

CHICKEN LIVER CHOW MEIN

Even if you don't usually like chicken livers you may like them in this liver and onion dish tossed with hot noodles. Try it substituting shredded sliced lamb kidneys (very fresh and soaked in ice water overnight) for the livers, and 1 cup mushrooms for the celery.

4 tablespoons bacon fat, or oil	2 tablespoons soy sauce
½ cup chopped onion	2 tablespoons cornstarch
¼ cup minced celery	4 tablespoons water
1 pound chicken livers, chopped	4 to 5 cups (8 ounces) cooked medium noodles
	¼ cup finely minced parsley

1. Measure fat, onions, celery, livers. Mix soy sauce and cornstarch with water. Set all ingredients by the stove in the order listed.

2. Set *wok* over high heat for 30 seconds, add *half* the fat, count to 20. Add onions; stir-fry until golden. Add celery and livers; stir-fry 4 to 5 minutes. Add soy and cornstarch mixture, and stir until sauce thickens and clears.

3. Set heavy skillet over high heat; melt remaining fat. Turn cooked noodles into skillet; fry until brown on underside. Turn, brown on other side. Place in serving dish. Pour contents of *wok* over noodles; sprinkle with parsley.

Serves 2 to 4, more if other dishes are offered.

LO MEIN WITH VEGETABLES

Crispy vegetables over heated cooked noodles, to serve with any strongly flavored meat dish. Almost any vegetable can be used if cut into sizes described. Place long-to-cook vegetables in *wok* first.

2 tablespoons bacon fat, or oil
¼ can bamboo shoots
1 packed cup fresh spinach
8 dried Chinese mushrooms, or fresh
2 tablespoons sauerkraut

2 to 3 cups (about 4 ounces) cooked medium noodles
2 tablespoons soy sauce
1 teaspoon cornstarch
1 cup mushroom water, or Beef Stock
2 tablespoons dry sherry
Salt and pepper to taste

1. Measure fat. Drain bamboo shoots, rinse in cold water and shred. Wash spinach. Cover dried mushrooms with boiling water, soak 20 minutes, drain, reserving water. Squeeze mushrooms dry and chop. If mushrooms are fresh, wipe clean and chop coarsely. Rinse and drain sauerkraut. Measure noodles. Mix soy sauce with cornstarch and 1 cup mushroom water. Arrange all ingredients by the stove in order listed.

2. Set *wok* over high heat for 30 seconds, swirl in fat, count to 20, add bamboo shoots, and stir-fry 2 minutes. Add spinach, mushrooms, sauerkraut, and stir-fry 3 minutes more. Add cooked egg noodles, and toss well. Push ingredients to one side, pour cornstarch mixture down side of *wok*, stir until it

thickens and clears, and mix all ingredients into sauce. Stir in sherry, salt and pepper to taste, and serve hot.

Serves 4 to 6.

TRANSPARENT NOODLES AND SHRIMP

Made of mung beans, transparent or cellophane noodles are a delicacy of Chinese cuisine and are available at specialty shops. Soak them in cold water for 30 minutes, then cover with boiling water. Return water to a boil, drain off, pour cold water over noodles and drain again.

2 tablespoons vegetable oil
1 small onion, minced
½ cup cooked pork, shredded
¼ cup dried Chinese mushrooms
1 cup raw shrimp, shelled, deveined, diced

1 tablespoon dry sherry
1 tablespoon soy sauce
Grated black pepper
½ cup celery, minced
½ cup mushroom water
2½ cups transparent noodles, prepared as above

1. Measure oil, mince onion, shred pork (I do it in the blender). Cover dried mushrooms with boiling water, and soak 20 minutes. Drain, reserving ½ cup water, squeeze dry, and cut into shreds. Measure balance of ingredients and set by the stove in the order listed.

2. Set *wok* over high heat for 30 seconds, swirl in the oil, count to 20, add onions; stir-fry until starting to brown, 3 to 4 minutes. Add pork and mushrooms; stir-fry 2 minutes. Add shrimp; stir-fry until color turns brighter pink. Add sherry; mix well. Add soy sauce and pepper; mix again. Add celery; stir-fry 2 minutes more. Pour mushroom water down the side of the *wok*, heat to a simmer, add noodles, toss to reheat, and serve.

Serves 2 to 4.

8. Tempura
and Other Fishy Delights

MOST ORIENTAL PEOPLE eat more fish than do Americans—perhaps because few of our inland waters are "farmed" and seafood even a day old can be much too "fishy." Just one poor package of frozen fish can put you off, which is unfortunate, since most raw frozen seafood is excellent, and doubly unfortunate because fish supplies phosphorus and Vitamin B, as well as the protein and amino acids which meats contain. And since fish are fed neither tranquilizers nor hormones and are not grazed on spray-poisoned meadows, their flesh is still relatively wholesome.

In Oriental diets fish is often more important than meat. It follows that the Oriental ways with fish are not only manifold but wonderfully inventive as well. A recipe calling for sugar, fish, sherry, ginger, scallions, and meat is enough to scare a Frenchwoman out of her wits, but the result is typically and delightfully Oriental. The potentiality of fish to flavor other foods superbly is so prized that most countries in the East have their own varieties of fish or oyster sauce with which to cook.

Because shrimp and lobster are popular, I keep these and raw crab in the freezer to make late snacks and impromptu meals. Egg Rolls, for instance, call for pork and shrimp. But don't, even if you love shrimp, add more than a recipe calls for. In moments of mad generosity, I have doubled seafood proportions and found the delicate balances of the Oriental recipe destroyed and the whole dish somehow wrong.

In the Orient, fish dishes are generally served with meat dishes. Of every set of three dishes in an Oriental meal, I always make one of fish.

SWEET-AND-SOUR SHRIMP

Sweet, crusty, deep-fried shrimp in a truly mouth-watering sauce. And it only takes about 30 minutes to make. Use all of the juice from a 16-ounce can of sweetened pineapple tidbits. Nice with Cantonese Fried Rice, which can be made ahead and kept warm.

1 cup flour	¼ cup water
1 teaspoon salt	1½ tablespoons oil
1 cup water	3 packed tablespoons
1 tablespoon oil	brown sugar, light
1 pound raw shrimp,	1½ teaspoons salt
shelled, deveined	¼ teaspoon black pepper
1 cup pineapple tidbits,	2 tablespoons vinegar
drained	1 tablespoon cornstarch
½ cup pineapple syrup	3 cups oil

1. In a medium bowl combine flour and salt. Mix in water and oil, and let rest for 20 minutes. Measure shrimp and pineapple. In a small saucepan, mix syrup, water, oil, sugar, salt, pepper, vinegar, cornstarch. Place batter, shrimp, pineapple and oil by stove. Turn oven to 250° and warm a serving dish lined with paper towel. Have handy a Chinese sieve or slotted spoon.

2. Set *wok* over high heat for 30 seconds, add 3 cups oil, heat to 350° on thermometer or until a drop of batter sizzles and rises to the surface. Mix shrimp into batter, scoop out

one at a time and drop into oil. Do only as many as can float freely at one time. Drain when golden brown, 2 to 3 minutes, and keep warm.

3. When all shrimp are done, simmer syrup mixture over medium heat, stirring, until it thickens and clears. Heat pineapple in syrup. Remove paper from serving dish, pour syrup and pineapple over shrimp and serve at once.

Serves 4, more if other dishes are offered.

TEMPURA DINNER, JAPAN

Batter-dipped seafood and vegetables. Serve with Tempura Sauce. The correct batter recipe calls for 2 cups flour, 2 eggs, 1½ cups water, but I much prefer the batter recipe below.

2 cups flour
2 teaspoons salt
1 teaspoon paprika
2 cups water less 4 tablespoons
2 tablespoons oil
1 tablespoon dry sherry
6 rock lobster tails, or 6 giant shrimp, raw
6 oysters or mussels or clams, raw
18 small sardines, raw, or any small fish such as blowfish

6 raw salmon roe (or omit)
6 large fresh mushroom caps
6 small raw eggplant
6 young beet leaves and stems
1 cup Beef Stock
¼ cup oyster sauce, or soy sauce
4 tablespoons dry sherry
1 teaspoon minced ginger, fresh
½ cup prepared horseradish
3 to 4 cups oil

1. Place flour in large bowl, and stir in salt, paprika, water, mixing with your fingers (it's easier). Stir in 2 tablespoons oil and 1 tablespoon sherry. Set by stove while you

prepare other ingredients. Wash lobster (or shrimp), shell, leaving tail on. Shell and rinse oysters (or mussels), drain. Halve cleaned sardines, leaving heads and tails on; if using blowfish, clean, skin, remove head, cut across grain into 1-inch pieces. Separate roe into lumps of similar size. Wipe mushroom caps; stem eggplant. Wash and dry beet leaves, leave the stems on. Combine Beef Stock, oyster sauce or soy sauce, 4 tablespoons sherry, and ginger, and place in 6 small sauce bowls. Place a round ball of horseradish in center; place dishes on dinner table. Gather all other ingredients by the stove, with a Chinese strainer or slotted spoon. Heat serving dish in 250° oven and line it with paper towel.

2. Set *wok* over high heat for 30 seconds, swirl in oil, heat to 350° or until drop of batter sizzles and rises. Coat fish and vegetables 1 piece at a time in batter, place in groups of 7 or 8 in hot oil and fry golden brown, 3 to 4 minutes or less. Be careful oil doesn't overheat and smoke. If batter thins because of liquid from fish, add a little flour. Add a little fresh oil to *wok* as level goes down. Drain cooked ingredients on paper towel in warm oven. Serve when all are ready.

Serves 6.

SASHIMI (RAW FISH), JAPAN

This is served with small side dishes of Japanese soy sauce (Kikkoman), mixed with grated prepared horseradish. The slices of tuna can also be pressed onto small ovals of Vinegared Rice (Chapter 6) and served with plain soy sauce.

½ pound raw fresh tuna
6 tablespoons Japanese soy
 sauce

Leaves of beefsteak plant
5 tablespoons prepared
 horseradish

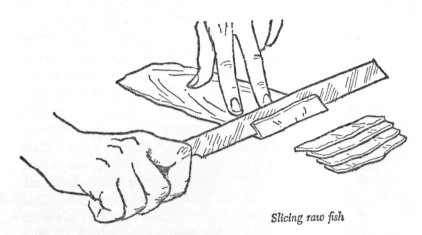

Slicing raw fish

Remove skin and bones, if any, from fish. With a very sharp knife slice fish into slanted pieces 1½ inches wide, ½ inch deep, and ¼ inch thick. If fish isn't firm enough to cut easily, freeze slightly. Arrange decoratively on serving plate with leaves of beefsteak plant, if available, and a little pile of horseradish. Serve with side dishes containing combined Japanese soy sauce and prepared horseradish.

Serves 2 to 4, more if other dishes are offered.

SHRIMP WITH BAMBOO SHOOTS, SZECHWAN

Szechwan is a district in China famous for a style of cooking that is rich with strong flavors, and FIERY. If you like Mexican food, you will like this type of cooking. I have cut down on chili powder and red pepper, and you might cut it in half again, or double or treble the quantities. Shrimp are marinated for 6 hours, so start early.

1 pound raw shrimp, shelled, deveined
1 egg white
1½ tablespoons cornstarch
½ cup bamboo shoots
2½ cups minced scallions
¼ teaspoon chili powder
¼ teaspoon red pepper flakes
1 tablespoon peeled chopped garlic
1 tablespoon minced fresh ginger, or 1½ teaspoons ground
½ cup Chicken Stock
5 tablespoons ketchup
½ teaspoon soy sauce
2 tablespoons dry sherry
½ teaspoon sesame oil (optional)
3 cups oil
2 tablespoons oil

1. In a medium bowl combine shrimp with egg white mixed with cornstarch. Marinate 6 hours.

2. In a medium bowl combine bamboo shoots, drained, rinsed, shredded, with scallions, chili powder, pepper, garlic, ginger. In blender on low combine Chicken Stock, ketchup, soy sauce, sherry, and sesame oil. Place these two mixtures and the marinated shrimp by the stove. Have handy a Chinese sieve or slotted spoon and a big sheet of paper towel.

3. Set *wok* over high heat for 30 seconds, pour in 3 cups oil, heat to 350° or until a drop of egg white sizzles. Slip shrimp 1 at a time into the oil and cook 1 minute without browning. Keep the cooking shrimp separated. Scoop out shrimp, drain on paper towel. The last step takes only a few minutes, so you can work on other portions of the meal while the oil cools, or else pour oil out immediately, wipe *wok* dry. Return to high heat for 30 seconds, add 2 tablespoons oil, heat while you count to 20. Add bamboo-shoot mixture; stir once. Add shrimp; stir-fry 2 minutes. Add Chicken Stock mixture and stir until shrimp are coated and mixture is hot. Serve at once with plain boiled rice. Offer salt at the table.

Serves 4, more if other dishes are offered.

GREEN BEANS AND SHRIMP, VIETNAM

To serve as part of a Vietnamese meal, or as a pleasant meal for two, with rice and a mild buttery salad.

2 tablespoons oil
1 small onion, chopped
1 pound raw shrimp, shelled, deveined
1 teaspoon salt

½ pound fresh green beans, Frenched, or 1 package frozen
2 tablespoons water
2 tablespoons fish sauce, or *Nuoc Mam*

1. Measure oil. Blender-chop onion. Slash shrimp down back so they are almost halved, but not quite. Measure salt. If beans are fresh, French-cut them, cover with boiling water for 1 minute, drain, dry with paper towel. Mix water and fish sauce. Gather ingredients by the stove in order listed.

2. Set *wok* over high heat for 30 seconds, swirl in oil, count to 20, add onion and stir-fry 1 minute. Add shrimp, salt, and toss well. Reduce heat to medium, stir-fry shrimp 1 minute. Add beans, stir-fry 3 minutes or less if frozen, a little longer if fresh. Color should be dark green. Pour fish sauce mixture down side of *wok*, stir and toss with ingredients until well blended and hot. Serve at once.

Serves 2 or 3, more if other dishes are offered.

SHRIMP PULAO, INDIA

Curry and saffron, raisins, almonds, shrimp—great texture and flavor combinations. Serve with chutney, diced apples, grated fresh coconut side dishes. Excellent for small patio parties. Easiest made with converted long-grain rice.

2 cups grated coconut, fresh or canned
3 cups boiling water
1 teaspoon oil
1 stick butter
3 medium onions, chopped
1 cup converted rice
2 cloves peeled garlic, minced
2 tablespoons slivered almonds
3 tablespoons seedless dark raisins
½ teaspoon ground cinnamon
4 cardamom seeds, peeled
¼ teaspoon ground mace
¼ teaspoon ground cloves
5 whole peppercorns
½ teaspoon ground ginger
Salt to taste
½ teaspoon saffron
16–20 ounces raw shrimp, shelled, deveined

1. Soak fresh coconut in boiling water for 30 minutes. If canned, rinse in cold water to eliminate sweet. Squeeze out coconut milk; reserve. Place shreds in serving dish and offer at table with Pulao when ready. Measure oil, butter, blender-chop onions, measure rice, mince garlic, measure almonds, raisins. Measure cinnamon, cardamom, mace, cloves, pepper-corns, ginger, and 1 teaspoon or more of salt into a small bowl. Assemble all ingredients by the stove.

2. Set *wok* over medium heat for 30 seconds, swirl in oil, melt butter. Add onions and stir-fry until golden, 3 to 4 minutes. Turn heat to low. Add rice; stir-fry 1 minute. Add all other ingredients except coconut milk, saffron, and shrimp. Stir simmering rice until it develops golden-opaque look, about 10 minutes. Stir in coconut milk, saffron, and shrimp. Cover

tightly, simmer 10 to 15 minutes, until rice is soft. Stir occasionally and add more water if rice is sticking.

Serves 4, more if other dishes are offered.

SHRIMP WITH VEGETABLES

This will serve 6 and is a fast, easy, one-dish patio dinner. Use frozen snow peas if available.

2 tablespoons oil
1 pound raw shrimp, shelled, deveined
1 cup Chinese cabbage, or other cabbage, shredded
½ pound mushrooms
1 cup peas, fresh or frozen
2 tablespoons shredded sweet peppers
4 scallions, shredded
1 clove peeled garlic, minced
1 cup Chicken Stock, or water
2 tablespoons soy sauce
½ cup slivered almonds
1 tablespoon cornstarch
½ cup water
6 cups boiled rice

1. Measure oil, rinse shrimp. Measure cabbage. Wipe mushrooms and slice into lengths ¼ inch thick. Dry peas if frozen and thawed. Prepare and measure peppers, scallions, garlic, and Chicken Stock, and place with soy sauce, almonds, and cornstarch dissolved in water by the stove in the order listed. Prepare rice and keep warm.

2. Set *wok* over high heat for 30 seconds, swirl in oil, count to 20, and add shrimp. Stir-fry 1 minute. Add cabbage, mushrooms, peas, peppers, scallions, garlic, stir-frying ½ minute after each addition. Pour Chicken Stock down side of *wok*, bring to simmer. Lower heat and simmer, covered, about 4 minutes, until peas are crispy tender. Season with soy sauce to taste. Stir in almonds. Pour cornstarch mixture down side of *wok* and stir until it thickens and clears. Serve at once.

Serves 6, more if other dishes are offered.

LOBSTER WITH BLACK BEANS, CANTON

Big chunks of lobster in a typically Cantonese sauce. South African frozen rock lobster tails are a good substitute for fresh lobster tails and in my area less expensive. Use two 9-ounce packages. Serve with rice.

¼ cup oil
2 teaspoons black beans, or soy sauce
2 cloves garlic, peeled, minced
¼ pound (½ cup) lean ground pork
1 tablespoon soy sauce
1 teaspoon salt
⅛ teaspoon ground ginger
Pinch MSG (optional)

½ teaspoon sugar
¼ teaspoon black pepper
1 scallion, minced, or 1 tablespoon minced onion
1 pound lobster tails, shelled
1 cup Chicken Stock, or water
2 tablespoons cornstarch
3 tablespoons water
2 eggs, slightly beaten

1. Measure and prepare ingredients as listed; cut lobster tails into 1-inch-thick slices across the grain. Mix cornstarch with water. Set ingredients by the stove in order listed and have handy a small bowl and a slotted spoon. Heat serving dish in 250° oven.

2. Set *wok* over high heat for 30 seconds, swirl in oil, count to 30, turn heat to medium. Add black beans and garlic, stir-fry until garlic begins to brown. Add pork and stir-fry 1 minute; remove to bowl with slotted spoon. Stir in soy sauce, salt, ginger, MSG, sugar, pepper, and scallion. Mix, then add lobster pieces and stir-fry 1 minute. Return pork to *wok*; mix. Swirl Chicken Stock and cornstarch mixture down side of *wok* and stir with juices until sauce begins to thicken and clear. Push solids to one side, dribble eggs into simmering sauce, stir and toss together all ingredients. Keep warm until ready to serve.

Serves 2 to 4, more as part of a large meal.

OYSTER CAKES

An unusual flavor combination—oysters and scallions—with a crispness that makes these little cakes a delightful extra at large Eastern meals. Nice as an appetizer, too.

4 eggs, slightly beaten
¼ cup oyster liquid
½ teaspoon salt
¼ teaspoon pepper
5 scallions, minced
4 tablespoons flour

½ teaspoon baking powder
1 pint (2 cups) shucked
　oysters, drained, chopped
3 cups oil
6 tablespoons vinegar
3 teaspoons chili sauce

1. In a medium bowl mix eggs, oyster liquid, salt, pepper, and scallions. Stir in flour and baking powder. Fold in chopped oysters. Place batter by the stove, with a Chinese sieve or a slotted spoon. Set paper-lined serving dish in 250° oven.

2. Set *wok* over high heat for 30 seconds, pour in oil, heat to 350° or until a drop of batter sizzles. Drop batter by tablespoonfuls into oil and fry golden brown, 2 or 3 minutes. Cook only as many as will float freely in oil at a time. Scoop out with sieve, drain, keep warm. Serve with vinegar and chili sauce combined.

Serves 4, more if other dishes are offered.

CRAB AND CUCUMBER CURRIED, INDIA

Seafood and cucumber are a popular combination in the East. We like this mild aromatic curry with rice. Takes about 30 minutes to prepare, 30 to cook, and makes a complete meal for 4. I use 3 packages frozen Alaska King crab. Start the rice, then begin.

¼ cup oil
1 large onion, chopped
1 clove peeled garlic,
  smashed
1 tablespoon ground
  coriander
½ teaspoon ground cumin
1 teaspoon turmeric
½ teaspoon ground ginger
½ teaspoon salt

½ cup (4 ounces) heavy
  cream
1 medium cucumber,
  peeled, in rounds ¼ inch
  thick
Milk
1 pound raw shelled
  crabmeat chunks
4 cups cooked rice

1. Measure and prepare ingredients and set by the stove in the order listed.

2. Set *wok* over medium heat for 30 seconds, swirl in oil, and count to 30. Add onion, stir-fry until golden, 3 to 4 minutes. Lower heat. Add garlic, coriander, cumin, turmeric, ginger, and salt. Stir and toss 10 minutes. Add cream and cucumber slices; simmer, stirring occasionally, until cucumber is tender, 3 to 4 minutes. Add milk if sauce dries out. Stir in crab, simmer 4 to 5 minutes, or until done. Serve over hot rice.

Serves 4.

STEAMED SEA BASS

This is a classic Chinese way of doing fish such as sea bass. If you haven't basket steamers, improvise as explained in Chapter 1. Black beans are available at Chinese specialty shops.

2 tablespoons black beans
1 tablespoon soy sauce
1 tablespoon dry sherry
1 tablespoon oil
½ teaspoon sugar

1½ pounds fresh sea bass,
  head and tail included
18 shreds fresh ginger root
1 scallion in shreds 2
  inches long

1. Chop black beans and mix in a small bowl with soy sauce, sherry, oil, and sugar. Wash and dry cleaned fish. Make ½-inch-deep slashes every half inch down the meatiest part of each side of fish, from gills to tail. Make slashes deepest where fish is thickest. Set fish on its side on an oven-proof serving dish that will fit steaming equipment. Arrange black bean mixture attractively down the side of the fish so that juices run into gashes, and beans cover them. Place ginger shreds over beans in a pattern of x's that touch at top and base. Divide scallion shreds into 4 or 5 bunches, each including some green, and arrange bunches decoratively over ginger pattern. Place dish inside steamer.

2. Fill steamer base with boiling water to within an inch of serving dish, bring water back to a rapid boil, cover, and steam fish 30 minutes, or until fish eye is white and protrudes. Add more water if necessary.

Serves 3 to 4, more if other dishes are offered.

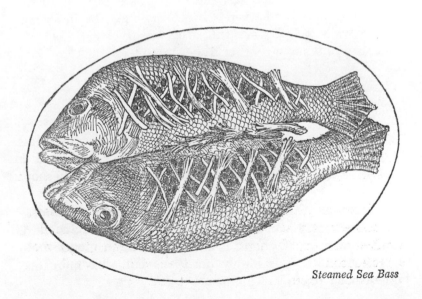

Steamed Sea Bass

SCALLOPS WITH PEPPERS

Pepper chunks are bright green, tender, but textured, and the quick-cooked scallop slices are deliciously "scallopy." We serve this with a mild fried rice.

2 tablespoons oil
1 small onion
2 to 3 cups raw scallops
½ teaspoon salt
¼ teaspoon black pepper
3 sweet peppers
1 tablespoon dry sherry

1. Measure oil. Slice peeled onion into thin rounds. Rinse scallops, drain well, slice into rounds ¼ inch thick. Measure salt, pepper, seed sweet peppers, rinse, cut into 1-inch squares. Place with sherry and all other ingredients by the stove in the order listed.

2. Set *wok* over high heat for 30 seconds, swirl in oil, count to 30, add onion, and stir-fry 1 minute. Add scallops, toss to coat with oil, add salt and pepper, and stir-fry 3 minutes. Add peppers and stir-fry 2 to 3 minutes. Stir in sherry. Remove while peppers are still deep green.

Serves 4 to 6, more if other dishes are offered.

WHITE FISH WITH BEAN CURD

This is not my favorite recipe, but it is a popular Chinese way with white fish and you might like to try it. Bean curd, available at specialty shops, is a cheesy substance made from soy bean "milk." It is highly nutritious but adds more texture than flavor, in my opinion.

2 tablespoons oil
1 pound flounder or
  haddock fillets
2 tablespoons dry sherry
1 teaspoon minced fresh
  ginger or ½ teaspoon
  ground

2 tablespoons soy sauce
1 scallion
½ cup water
1 teaspoon salt
2 squares bean curd
½ cup cooked peas

1. Measure oil. Cut fish into 1-inch cubes. Measure sherry, ginger, soy sauce. Cut scallion into 1-inch lengths. Measure water, salt, and cut bean curd into ½-inch cubes. Place peas and all other ingredients by the stove in order listed.

2. Set *wok* over medium-high heat for 30 seconds, swirl in oil, count to 20, turn heat to medium low. Add fish and stir-fry until brown on all sides, about 3 minutes. Add sherry, ginger, soy sauce, scallion, water, and salt. Simmer 1 minute. Add bean curd, stir-fry briefly, then simmer 4 minutes. Stir in peas. Serve hot.

Serves 4, more if other dishes are offered.

FLOUNDER, INDIA

Curry-flavored flounder fillets crisped in hot oil. We like it with a vegetable curry that includes potato, and with side dishes of crisp vegetables and chutney.

1 pound flounder fillets
1 tablespoon lemon juice,
  strained
1½ teaspoons salt
2 teaspoons curry powder
4 tablespoons flour

¼ teaspoon chili powder
¼ teaspoon black pepper
½ teaspoon salt
½ cup warm water
2 teaspoons minced parsley
3 cups oil

1. Separate flounder into small, thin fillets. Wipe dry, dredge with lemon juice, salt, and curry. Stir flour, chili powder,

pepper, and salt into water, and add *half* the parsley. Place oil, fish fillets, batter by the stove, along with a Chinese sieve or slotted spoon. Line serving platter with paper towel and set in 250° oven.

2. Set *wok* over high heat for 30 seconds, add oil and heat to 375° or until a day-old cube of bread browns (about 1 minute). Coat fillets lightly with batter, slide into oil, cook until golden, 2 to 3 minutes. Only do as many at a time as *wok* will float. Remove gently with sieve, drain, keep warm until all are done. Remove paper from serving dish, arrange fillets decoratively, garnish with remaining parsley, and serve at once.

Serves 2 to 3, more if other dishes are offered.

FLOUNDER WITH PINEAPPLE

Crisp soy-and-sherry-flavored flounder with pineapple chunks in a sweet-and-sour sauce. We like this with a curry and rice.

2 tablespoons soy sauce
½ teaspoon salt
1 tablespoon dry sherry
1 scallion, shredded
1½ pounds flounder fillets
2 tablespoons cornstarch
2 tablespoons water

2 eggs, slightly beaten
3 tablespoons oil
⅓ cup pineapple syrup
1 tablespoon sugar
1 cup pineapple chunks, unsweetened

1. In a medium bowl mix soy sauce, salt, sherry, scallion, and flounder cut into 1½-inch chunks. Place by stove with cornstarch mixed with water and eggs in a large, flat-bottomed bowl. Have handy oil, pineapple syrup, sugar, and pineapple chunks, drained. Place serving dish lined with paper towel in oven at 250°.

2. Set *wok* over high heat for 30 seconds, swirl in oil, count to 20. Dip each fish chunk in cornstarch mixture, toss into

oil and stir-fry about 4 minutes; transfer to heated serving dish. Add syrup to remaining cornstarch, mix, turn into *wok* with sugar and fruit chunks. Stir till sauce thickens and clears. If too thick, add a little more syrup or water. Remove paper from serving dish, pour sauce over fish chunks, and serve at once.

Serves 4 to 6, more if other dishes are offered.

SWEET-AND-SOUR FISH

A milder version of Spice Sauce with Fish Chunks (Chapter 3). Use haddock or cod, frozen or fresh. We like this with a fried rice and Egg Rolls.

2 tablespoons oil	¼ cup seeded, grated sweet
2 tablespoons vinegar	pepper
1½ teaspoons sugar	1 cup flour
2 tablespoons water	1 cup water, minus 2
¼ teaspoon salt	tablespoons
2 tablespoons ketchup	1 tablespoon oil
¼ cup coarse grated carrot	1 teaspoon salt
1 small tomato, peeled,	1 pound white fish fillets
chopped	3 cups oil

1. In a small saucepan combine oil, vinegar, sugar, water, salt, ketchup, and simmer over medium heat, stirring occasionally until sauce thickens slightly, 3 to 5 minutes. Add carrot, tomato, pepper, a little at a time so sauce continues to simmer. When vegetables look wilted, 2 to 3 minutes or less, turn off heat.

2. Place flour in medium bowl, stir in water, oil, salt. Cut fish into 1-inch cubes. Place batter and fish by the stove with oil, and a Chinese sieve or slotted spoon. Set paper-lined serving dish in oven at 250°.

3. Set *wok* over high heat for 30 seconds, add oil, heat to

350°, or until drop of batter sizzles and rises. Fry fish chunks dipped in batter 7 or 8 at a time, drain well, keep warm in oven. When all are done, reheat sauce, adding a little water if too thick. Remove paper from serving dish, pour sauce over fish chunks, and serve at once.

Serves 4, more if other dishes are offered.

FISH CURRY, INDIA

A dry aromatic curry made in minutes, nice as part of a larger meal. Use flounder fillets, haddock, cod, or any white fish.

1½ pounds fish fillets
2 teaspoons minced onion
⅛ teaspoon chili powder
½ teaspoon turmeric
¼ teaspoon ground coriander
¼ teaspoon ground cumin

⅛ teaspoon ground aniseed
1 clove garlic, peeled, minced
2 teaspoons salt
2 tablespoons oil

1. Cut fish into pieces 2 inches long by 1 inch wide, and toss with onion, chili, turmeric, coriander, cumin, aniseed, garlic, and salt. Let stand 1 hour.

2. Set *wok* over high heat for 30 seconds, swirl in oil, count to 20, add fish and stir gently 3 to 5 minutes until fish looks opaque. Add a little oil if dish is dry. Serve at once.

Serves 4, more if other dishes are offered.

LITTLE FRIED FISH

Eat these head, tail, and all. If you aren't partial to the special flavor of sesame oil, use salt instead. Can be the crisp part of a multi-dish meal, or an appetizer. Use any flavorful fish about 6 inches long.

8 to 12 small fish
½ cup soy sauce
½ tablespoon dry sherry
¼ teaspoon ground anise
 seed

⅛ teaspoon ground ginger
3 cups oil
1 tablespoon sesame oil

1. Clean fish without removing head or tail, and scale gently. Soak in soy sauce mixed with sherry, anise, and ginger for 30 minutes. Wipe fish with paper towel, and set by stove with oil and a sieve or slotted spoon. Place serving dish lined with paper towel in oven at 250°.

2. Set *wok* over high heat for 30 seconds, add oil, heat to 350° or until a bit of bread sizzles when it hits the oil. Lower fish into oil, as many as *wok* will hold comfortably, and fry until crisp and brown, about 5 minutes. Drain, keep warm, and sprinkle with a few drops sesame oil just before serving.

Serves 4, more as part of a larger meal.

TUNA WITH SAFFRON AND RICE, VIETNAM

This is a distinctly different tuna dish. Fish sauce, or *Nuoc Mam*, is sold at specialty shops.

1 pound fresh tuna
½ teaspoon saffron
½ teaspoon salt
1 teaspoon fish sauce
 (*Nuoc Mam*)
¼ teaspoon chili powder

1 clove garlic, peeled,
 smashed
3 tablespoons heavy cream
2 tablespoons oil
2 cups rice

1. Shred skinned, boned tuna, toss with saffron, salt, fish sauce, and chili powder, and marinate ½ hour. Measure

garlic, cream, oil. Cook rice and keep warm in serving dish. Set oil, garlic, spiced fish, and heavy cream in that order by the stove.

2. Set *wok* over high heat for 30 seconds, swirl in oil, count to 30, add garlic, stir-fry until clove begins to brown. Lower heat to medium, remove clove, add fish, and stir-fry 2 minutes. Push fish to one side, pour cream down *wok* side, mix with pan juices, then stir in fish. Simmer 2 minutes, stirring occasionally. Pour over rice, serve at once.

Serves 2 to 4, more if other dishes are offered.

FISH BALLS, BURMA

Spicy, nice with plain rice and chutney. Use flounder, cod, or haddock fillets, fresh or frozen.

2 pounds fish fillets	1 teaspoon curry
3 medium onions, minced	2 teaspoons salt
4 cloves garlic, peeled, minced	Flour
¼ teaspoon chili powder	½ cup oil
1 teaspoon grated lemon rind	3 medium tomatoes, peeled, chopped

1. Cut fish into chunks, place ⅓ at a time in blender and grind. In a small bowl combine onion, garlic, chili, lemon rind, curry, and salt. Line a soup bowl with about an inch of flour.

2. Set *wok* over medium heat for 30 seconds, swirl in *half* the oil, count to 30, add onion mixture, and stir-fry until onion is golden, 2 to 3 minutes. With a slotted spoon return mixture to mixing bowl. Turn off heat.

3. Stir ⅓ of onion mixture into ground fish, reserving balance. Roll between palms into balls the size of a small cherry tomato, then roll in flour until well coated.

4. Just before dinner, turn heat under *wok* to medium high

for 30 seconds, add remaining oil, count to 20, add fish balls in lots the *wok* handles comfortably, and fry golden brown on all sides. Keep warm. You may need a little more oil. When all are done, stir tomatoes into juices in the *wok* and scrape up sauce, adding a little water if necessary. Add reserved onion mixture, and simmer 10 minutes, until tomatoes have cooked down. Serve over hot fish.

Serves 4 to 6, more if other dishes are offered.

9. Instant Meats and Marvelous Mixtures

TWO OF THE greatest gifts of Eastern cuisine are the very rapid preparation of meat dishes and their wide range of delicate flavors. The meats are quite familiar to us, but they are cooked with a little shrimp or spices or a sweet-and-sour sauce, and—presto—they are altogether different.

In China, pork and chicken predominate on the menu. In India, lamb and beef are used more often. Indian meats cook quickly too, though they are not flash-cooked. The diversity in curry flavors comes primarily from the proportions and combinations in which the many spices are used. Curry (meats are nearly always curried) is not a spice. It is a powder containing a number of ground spices—up to twenty-nine, but generally fewer. The most common mixtures include coriander, cumin, ginger, garlic, and turmeric for color. Fresh-ground, they remind the nose not at all of curry powders purchased here.

Curry dishes vary in their content as well as in their spices. *Kormas* are yogurt-based, and my favorites. *Vindaloos* are vinegared. *Molees* are made with coconut milk. Some curries are dry, some are moist. Rice is served with curries along with small strongly flavored side dishes such as grated fresh coconut, apples diced with lemon juice, chopped onions (see *Raita*), minced chilies, cucumbers mixed with yogurt (see *Sambal*). Chutney (*Achar*), hot or sweet, is served with curry.

Major Grey is a popular brand in America; and the chutneys from Chutney Kitchen, in Yountville, California, are extraordinarily good.

The mainstay of the Chinese meal is a meat, fish, or vegetable dish, or all three. In India, it is a curry dish—meat, fish, or vegetable.

Pork

BARBECUED SPARERIBS

This is a rather dry form of spareribs. It is important that it cook long enough, otherwise the flavor will be poor. Use as an appetizer or as part of a larger meal. Halve the garlic, if you like.

2½ pounds spareribs
1 cup soy sauce
½ cup pineapple juice
¼ cup dry sherry

1½ tablespoons packed light brown sugar
4 cloves garlic, peeled, crushed

1. Cut spareribs into 2-inch sections. Place in a large bowl. Combine remaining ingredients, mix with spareribs and marinate ribs 6 hours at room temperature, turning often.

2. Turn broiler to medium. Place rack 15 inches from fire, and set rib sections under the fire on a Teflon-lined tray. Broil ribs 7 minutes on the upper side, basting frequently; turn, broil and baste 10 minutes on that side. Turn oven to 300°. Place ribs in oven, baste again with marinade, and allow to finish cooking for 20 to 30 minutes.

Serves 4 to 6.

SWEET-AND-SOUR MEAT BALLS

These are the Meat Balls from Chapter 3, half the recipe, which I reserve and freeze to serve in this sauce, made with carrots, green pepper, and chunks of pineapple. *Very good.* When I am short of the frozen Meat Balls, I add a few rolled, fried hamburger balls.

12 to 18 Meat Balls, raw
1½ tablespoons oil
Juice from 16-ounce can
  unsweetened pineapple
  chunks
3 teaspoons light brown
  sugar
½ teaspoon salt

¼ teaspoon pepper
2 tablespoons white vinegar
2 long thin carrots
1 green pepper
2 cups unsweetened
  pineapple chunks
1 tablespoon cornstarch
¼ cup water

1. Prepare (or thaw) and deep-fry Meat Balls (page 39, half the recipe or a little more). Keep warm in paper-lined serving dish in 250° oven.

2. Measure oil. Combine in a small bowl pineapple juice, brown sugar, salt, pepper, vinegar. Wash carrots, slice in thinnest rounds. Wash and seed green pepper, cut into thinnest shreds, or grate on coarse side of grater. Measure pineapple chunks, mix cornstarch with water. Set all ingredients by the stove in the order listed, except the Meat Balls.

3. Set *wok* over high heat for 30 seconds, swirl in oil, count to 20, add pineapple juice mixture and bring to a boil. Add carrots; stir, cover, cook 3 minutes. Add peppers; stir-fry 1 minute. Add meat balls and pineapple chunks; toss to heat through, push to one side. Pour cornstarch mixture down side of *wok*, stir till smooth and clear. Mix, serve hot.

Serves 4, more when other dishes are offered.

SWEET-AND-SOUR PORK

Similar to Sweet-and-Sour Meat Balls but faster, not quite so good.

2 pounds boneless pork
2 tablespoons dry sherry
3 to 4 tablespoons soy
  sauce
4 tablespoons cornstarch
3 cups oil
2 tablespoons oil
1 large sweet onion
2 sweet peppers
1 carrot
½ cup water chestnuts,
  diced

2 cups pineapple chunks,
  unsweetened
Pineapple syrup
3 teaspoons light brown
  sugar
½ teaspoon salt
¼ teaspoon pepper
2 tablespoons white vinegar
1 tablespoon cornstarch
¼ cup water

1. Cut pork into 1-inch cubes, toss with sherry and soy sauce, marinate 10 minutes, dredge in cornstarch. Measure 3 cups oil, and 2 tablespoons oil into separate bowls. Cut onion into 8 wedges. Seed and wash peppers, cut into shreds ½ inch wide. Wash carrot, slice into thinnest rounds. Measure water chestnuts, pineapple chunks. Combine in a small bowl the syrup, sugar, salt, pepper, and vinegar. Mix cornstarch with water. Place ingredients by stove in order listed, along with a sieve or slotted spoon. Set paper-lined serving dish in 250° oven.

2. Set *wok* over high heat for 30 seconds, add 3 cups oil, heat to 350° or until a bit of bread sizzles when it hits the oil. Brown pork cubes a third at a time, 4 to 5 minutes. Keep warm. Pour off oil, return *wok* to high heat. Add 2 tablespoons oil, count to 30, add onions, stir-fry 2 minutes, but do not brown. Add carrots; stir-fry 2 minutes. Add peppers; stir-fry 2 minutes. Add pineapple-juice mixture, pouring

down side of *wok,* and stir until it simmers. Add water chestnuts and pineapple; mix. Push ingredients to one side; pour cornstarch mixture down side of *wok,* stir until sauce thickens and clears. Mix with vegetables. Remove paper liner from serving dish, pour sauce and vegetables over pork cubes. Serve hot.

Serves 6 to 8, more if other dishes are offered.

PORK ROLLS IN LETTUCE

Choose a soft, not a crisp, lettuce for this, such as Boston or Bibb. Prepare filling ahead, keep warm, and stuff lettuce wrappers just before serving. Number of rolls you can make depends on size of lettuce leaves.

1 tablespoon oil	1 tablespoon dry sherry
1½ pounds ground pork	½ cup minced celery
¾ teaspoon salt	2 scallions, minced
1 teaspoon sugar	12 or more lettuce leaves
1 tablespoon soy sauce	

1. Measure oil. Mix pork with salt, sugar, and soy sauce. Measure sherry. Mince celery, scallions. Wash lettuce leaves, and dry. Place ingredients by the stove in order listed.

2. Set *wok* over high heat for 30 seconds. Add oil, count to 20, add pork, and stir-fry 2 minutes. Add sherry; stir-fry until pork is brown and crumbly. Mix in celery and scallions, toss; keep warm until ready to scrve.

3. Spoon portions of hot pork onto lettuce leaves, roll as Egg Rolls. If necessary, spear rolls with toothpicks to keep together.

Serves 6, more if other dishes are offered.

PORK CHOP-SUEY

A good patio recipe. We like it served with boiled medium-broad noodles.

2 tablespoons oil
1 pound lean pork,
   shredded
2 tablespoons oil
1 cup blender-chopped
   onion
12 dried Chinese
   mushrooms, or fresh
   mushrooms
3 stalks celery
1 medium sweet pepper

2 to 3 tablespoons soy
   sauce
1 cup bean sprouts
8 water chestnuts
1 teaspoon fresh minced
   ginger, or ½ teaspoon
   ground
2 cups mushroom water, or
   Beef Stock
1 tablespoon cornstarch
3 tablespoons water

1. Measure oil, shred pork. Measure oil, blender-chop onion. Cover dried mushrooms with boiling water, enough to make 2 cups, and soak 20 minutes. Drain, reserving water. Mince mushrooms. Or cut fresh mushrooms into lengths ¼ inch thick. Cut celery in rounds ¼ inch thick. Wash and seed pepper, shred. Measure soy sauce. Drain and rinse bean sprouts. Chop water chestnuts. Mince fresh ginger. Measure mushroom water, or Beef Stock. Mix cornstarch with water. Place all ingredients by stove in order listed, along with a small bowl and a slotted spoon.

2. Set *wok* over high heat for 30 seconds, swirl in oil, count to 30, add pork shreds, and stir-fry 4 to 5 minutes. Use slotted spoon to scoop into bowl. Add 2 tablespoons oil to *wok*, count to 10, add onions, toss with oil. Add mushrooms; stir-fry 2 minutes. Add celery and pepper; stir-fry 1 minute. Add soy sauce; mix well. Add bean sprouts, water chestnuts, ginger and mushroom water. Stir-cook 2 minutes. Return pork shreds to mixture, mix well, push in-

gredients to one side. Pour cornstarch mixture down side of *wok*, stir until it thickens and clears. Toss with other ingredients, and serve hot. Offer soy at the table.

Serves 6, with noodles, more if other dishes are offered.

PORK AND NUTS IN SWEET SAUCE

Use skinned unroasted cashews for this, or peanuts; many health-food stores carry them, organically grown and ready to go.

2 tablespoons oil	2 green peppers, seeded, diced
1 pound pork, shredded	
2 tablespoons soy sauce	1½ tablespoons light brown sugar
2 medium carrots, coarse-grated	
½ cup skinned blanched nuts	1 tablespoon cornstarch
	3 tablespoons water
	Salt to taste

1. Measure and prepare ingredients and set by stove in order listed.

2. Set *wok* over high heat for 30 seconds, swirl in oil, heat for long enough to count to 30. Add pork; stir-fry until it begins to brown, 2 to 3 minutes. Sprinkle with soy sauce; stir-fry 1 minute. Turn heat to medium, add carrots, mix, cover, cook 1 minute. Add nuts and peppers; stir-fry 3 to 4 minutes. Add sugar, mix till sugar melts. Push ingredients to one side, pour cornstarch mixed with water down side of *wok*, stir till sauce thickens and clears. Mix well, salt to taste, and serve hot.

Serves 4 to 6, more if other dishes are offered.

PORK CURRY, INDIA

A creamy pork dish we like with saffron rice and a crispy vegetable. Serve with chutney. Pork marinates for 2 hours, so start early.

1 teaspoon oil
½ cup (1 stick) butter
1 large onion, chopped
1 green chili, seeded,
  chopped (optional)
2 tablespoons tomato paste
½ cup white vinegar
½ teaspoon turmeric
1 teaspoon ground ginger

1 teaspoon ground
  coriander
½ teaspoon salt
1 pound pork in 1½-inch
  cubes
½ pint plain yogurt
½ teaspoon salt
⅛ teaspoon black pepper

1. Measure oil and butter, prepare onion and chili, and measure tomato paste. In a small bowl mix vinegar, turmeric, ginger, coriander, and salt. In a large bowl mix pork with yogurt, salt, and pepper, and marinate for 2 hours. Set ingredients by the stove in order listed.

2. Set *wok* over medium heat for 30 seconds, swirl oil to coat sides, melt butter, and stir-fry onion until golden, 3 to 4 minutes. Add chili and tomato paste; stir-fry 1 minute. Add vinegar mixed with spices, stir, simmer 5 minutes. Lower heat if cooking too quickly. Add pork and yogurt mixture, cover, cook over medium to low heat 40 minutes until pork is tender. Check to make sure sauce isn't sticking. If sauce is too thin, cook uncovered last 10 minutes.

Serves 3 to 4, with rice.

MEAT LOAF, VIETNAM

A small steamed meat loaf, quite different from the American kind. Serves 4 as part of a larger meal. If you don't have steaming equipment, improvise as described in Chapter 1. Bean thread is available at specialty shops.

1 package bean thread
8 dried Chinese mushrooms
1 pound ground pork
½ teaspoon salt
¼ teaspoon pepper
1 teaspoon fish sauce
  (*Nuoc Mam*), or soy
  sauce, or oyster sauce

3 cloves garlic, peeled,
  minced
3 shallots or 1 small onion,
  minced
4 eggs, slightly beaten

1. Cover bean thread with boiling water, soak 20 minutes, drain, chop, measure out ½ cup. Put balance aside for other use. Cover dried mushrooms with boiling water, soak 20 minutes. Drain, squeeze dry.

2. Place pork in large bowl, break lightly with fork. Sprinkle pieces with salt, pepper, mix. Add fish sauce, toss well, add garlic, shallots, and chopped bean thread, and mix well. Make well in center, pour eggs into it, and beat the pork into the eggs. Shape into meat loaf, place in ovenproof dish, set on floor of steamer. Add boiling water to steamer base, place over high heat, and wet-steam over rapidly boiling water 5 minutes.

Serves 4, more if other dishes are offered.

GREEN BEANS, FUKIEN

A family favorite. Serve with batter-dipped deep-fried shrimp (as Shrimp Tempura) and plain rice.

2 tablespoons oil
1 clove garlic, peeled,
  minced
1 pound lean ground pork
2 tablespoons soy sauce
¼ teaspoon salt
6 water chestnuts, slivered,
  or ½ cup diced celery

3 cups fresh green beans,
  in roll-cut diagonals
1½ cups boiling water
1 tablespoon cornstarch
¼ cup cold water
½ small head iceberg
  lettuce, shredded

1. Measure and prepare ingredients, mix cornstarch with ¼ cup cold water. Set all but lettuce by the stove in the order listed.

2. Set *wok* over high heat for 30 seconds, swirl in oil, count to 30, add garlic, stir quickly a few seconds. Add pork, and stir-fry until brown and crumbly. Add soy sauce, salt, water chestnuts, and stir-fry 2 minutes. Add beans; stir-fry 2 to 3 minutes. Pour water in thin stream down side of *wok*, toss mixture, cover, bring to a boil and turn down heat. Simmer 2 minutes, stirring occasionally. Beans should still be dark green, tender but crisp when removed. One minute before beans are done, add cornstarch, pouring down side of *wok*. Stir until sauce thickens, test beans, and cook another minute if necessary. Don't overcook. Serve hot on shredded lettuce.

Serves 4 to 6, more if many dishes are offered.

Beef

SUKIYAKI

One of the best-known Japanese recipes, and a great dish for casual patio entertaining. Cooking is done at the table in a large skillet, and diners help themselves from the simmering

Sukiyaki

dish. As contents of pan are depleted more are added and cooked. Don't cook vegetables to the point where their crispness and color are gone.

4 medium carrots, shredded
2 medium onions, in thin rounds
2 bunches green onions, in 1-inch roll-cut diagonals
1 medium bunch celery, in roll-cut diagonals
4 ounces mushroom caps, in slices ½ inch thick
10 ounces canned bamboo shoots
½ cup oil
2 pounds sirloin

1 package bean thread, or 8 ounces cooked vermicelli
2 squares bean curd (optional)
4 cups washed spinach pieces
2 cups Beef Stock
¾ cup Japanese soy sauce, or soy sauce
¼ cup sugar
3 tablespoons dry sherry
Raw eggs (optional)

1. Wash and cut carrots, onions, green onions, celery, mushrooms. Drain and rinse bamboo shoots. Measure oil into small pitcher. Cut sirloin into shreds 2 inches by 1 inch wide by ¼ inch thick. Soak bean thread in hot water 20 minutes, or cook

vermicelli until barely tender. Cube bean curd, and measure spinach. In a larger pitcher mix Beef Stock, soy sauce, sugar, and sherry. In the center of a very large platter arrange a row of bean thread and set meat slices on top. Place carrots on one side in a row, celery on the other. Arrange remaining vegetables in similar rows. Bring to the table with oil, sauce, and small bowls containing 1 slightly beaten egg for each diner.

2. Heat electric skillet to 350°, or heat large heavy skillet over high flame or hot coals. Add enough oil to just coat skillet bottom, heat until almost smoking, then lay meat pieces flat, and brown each side quickly, 1 or 2 minutes. Push meat to one side, and at once add about ⅓ of the sauce. Scrape up pan juices, quickly, and add ⅓ (or whatever the pan holds comfortably) of carrots, onions, green onions, celery, mushrooms, and bamboo shoots, and bring ingredients to a boil. Add more sauce if skillet seems dry. Place a portion of bean thread, bean curd, and raw spinach over vegetables, top with meat. When everything is boiling once more, guests help themselves, picking out whatever they want, and dipping each morsel into individual bowls of raw egg before eating.

Serves 4 to 6.

CHOP SUEY CHIMNEY HILL

One of my favorite uses for leftover beef roast, especially undercooked beef, and a popular one-dish family dinner. A good patio meal, too. Best made in a 14-inch *wok*, or a large cast-iron skillet.

2 tablespoons oil	½ pound mushrooms
1 medium onion, chopped	3 tablespoons butter
1 clove garlic, peeled,	(optional)
minced	1 to 2 cups beef shreds
4 medium stalks celery	3 tablespoons soy sauce
1 medium sweet pepper	1 tablespoon cornstarch
1 cup bean sprouts	¼ cup water

1. Measure oil, blender-chop onion, mince garlic. Cut celery and seeded sweet pepper into shreds 2 inches long by ⅛ or ¼ inch thick. Drain and rinse sprouts, measure. Wipe mushrooms, cut into lengths ⅛ inch thick. Measure butter. Cut beef into shreds 2 inches long by 1 inch wide by ¼ inch thick, and measure. Prepare soy sauce, and mix cornstarch with water. Set all ingredients by stove in order listed.

2. Set *wok* over high heat for 30 seconds, add oil, count to 20. Add onion and garlic; stir-fry 1 minute. Add celery and stir-fry until green brightens, 1 to 2 minutes. Add pepper; stir-fry 1 minute. Add bean sprouts; stir-fry 1 minute. Make space in center of *wok*, add mushrooms, stir half a minute, add butter and stir-fry until softened—about 2 minutes. Push mushrooms to one side, add beef and stir until warmed through. Sprinkle soy sauce over ingredients, pour cornstarch mixture down side of *wok*, mix in all ingredients and stir until sauce has thickened and cleared. Celery should still have crispness, peppers be dark green. Serve at once.

Serves 6, with rice.

BEEF SHREDS STIR-FRIED WITH ONIONS

One of our favorite Oriental dishes with beef—and nice even when made with less expensive steaks and chucks.

1½ pounds beef	½ teaspoon salt
1 teaspoon baking soda	1 medium onion, chopped
2 tablespoons soy sauce	4 tablespoons oil
1 tablespoon cornstarch	⅛ teaspoon pepper
2 tablespoons oil	Chinese parsley (optional)
1 tablespoon oil	

1. Cut beef into slices 2 inches long by 1 inch wide by ¼ inch thick. In a medium bowl toss beef slices with soda, and let stand 15 minutes. Mix soy sauce, cornstarch, and 2 tablespoons oil in a small bowl. Toss beef with this mixture,

and marinate 10 minutes more. Set marinated beef by stove with all other ingredients, measured and prepared, along with a slotted spoon and a small bowl.

2. Set *wok* over high heat for 30 seconds, swirl in 1 table-spoon oil, add salt, count to 30. Add onion and stir-fry 2 minutes. Remove onion with slotted spoon to bowl. Add 4 tablespoons oil to the *wok*, count to 30, add meat, and pepper, add parsley if desired, and stir-fry until color turns gray. Return cooked onion to *wok* and mix well with beef. Turn into serving dish and serve at once.

Serves 4 to 6, more if other dishes are offered.

HAMBURGER AND MUSHROOMS WITH SCALLIONS

A sharply flavored dish, crumbly in texture, to serve on a bed of crisp shredded lettuce. We like Sweet-and-Sour Sauce with it. Nice with noodles or rice, and a multiple vegetable dish.

2 tablespoons oil	1 tablespoon oyster sauce,
2 cloves garlic, peeled,	or soy sauce
smashed	2 tablespoons oil
2 scallions, chopped, or 1	½ pound mushrooms
tablespoon minced onion	2 teaspoons soy sauce
1 pound hamburger	1 cup shredded crisp
	lettuce

1. Measure oil. Prepare garlic, scallions, and hamburger, and set by the stove with measured oyster sauce, 2 more tablespoons oil, mushrooms wiped and sliced into lengths ¼ inch thick, and measured soy sauce, in the order listed. Have handy a slotted spoon and a small bowl. Measure lettuce.

2. Set *wok* over high heat for 30 seconds, swirl in 2 table-spoons oil, count to 30, add garlic and scallions, stir-fry 2

minutes. Add hamburger, break into bits, mix well with scallions, and stir-fry until brown and crumbly, 2 to 3 minutes. Sprinkle with oyster sauce; stir-fry 1 minute more, remove to a small bowl. Add 2 tablespoons oil to the *wok*, count to 20, add mushrooms and stir-fry until they soften, 2 to 3 minutes. Add soy sauce, mix well. Return meat to *wok*, toss with mushrooms 1 to 2 minutes, until heated through. Keep warm until ready to serve, then line serving plate with lettuce, pour meat mixture over it, and serve at once.

Serves 4, more if other dishes are offered.

CUBED BEEF WITH OYSTER SAUCE

Very meaty flavor. Serve with plain rice and crisp vegetables in a sauce.

1 pound bottom round	½ cup oyster sauce
3 tablespoons oil	2 teaspoons sugar
1 clove garlic, peeled, smashed	1 tablespoon dry sherry
½ teaspoon salt	2 cups boiling water
3 tablespoons soy sauce	4 scallions, chopped

1. Cut beef into 1-inch cubes; cut across the grain where there are tough membranes. Prepare and measure all other ingredients and set by stove in order listed.

2. Set *wok* over high heat for 30 seconds, swirl in oil, count to 30, add garlic, salt, count to 5. Add beef; stir-fry until browned on all sides, 3 to 4 minutes. Add soy sauce; stir quickly. Add oyster sauce, sugar, sherry; stir again. Pour boiling water down side of *wok*, mix into beef, cover, turn down heat and simmer 25 minutes, or until sauce is cooked down and thickened. Add scallions, stir until they are dark green. Serve as soon as possible.

Serves 4, more if other dishes are offered.

BEEF STIR-FRIED WITH SNOW PEAS

Nice with Sweet-and-Sour Shrimp, a stir-fried mushroom dish, and rice.

4 tablespoons oil
1 clove garlic, peeled,
　smashed
½ pound bottom round
1 tablespoon dry sherry
1 tablespoon soy sauce
2 tablespoons cornstarch

2 tablespoons oil
¼ pound fresh snow peas
　or 1 package frozen,
　thawed
2 tablespoons soy sauce
½ teaspoon sugar

1. Measure oil, prepare garlic. Cut beef into slices 2 inches long by 1 inch wide by ¼ inch thick, sprinkle with sherry and soy sauce, and mix with cornstarch. Measure 2 tablespoons oil. String fresh snow peas and boil until half tender (or dry thawed snow peas). Measure soy, sugar, and set all ingredients by the stove in order listed with a slotted spoon, and a small bowl.

2. Set *wok* over high heat for 30 seconds, swirl in oil, count to 20, add garlic, stir once or twice, add beef, and stir-fry until color has changed. Remove to bowl. Add 2 tablespoons oil, count to 5, add snow peas and stir-fry 1 minute or 2, until tender but still crisp. Return beef to *wok*, sprinkle with 2 tablespoons soy sauce and sugar, stir-fry 1 minute more, serve hot.

Serves 4, more if other dishes are offered.

KOFTA (MEAT BALL) CURRY, INDIA

Delicious and inexpensive fare for patio parties. A one-dish dinner to serve with rice, chutney, and salad.

2 pounds ground beef
1 tablespoon ground coriander
5 cloves garlic, peeled, minced
1 teaspoon ground cloves
2 teaspoons minced ginger, fresh, or 1 teaspoon ground ginger
1 teaspoon ground cumin
½ teaspoon salt

1 egg, slightly beaten
1 teaspoon oil
1 stick (½ cup) butter
2 large onions, peeled, sliced in rounds
1 tablespoon tomato paste
1 pint plain yogurt
5 cardamom seeds, peeled
1 cup water
½ teaspoon saffron
⅛ cup water

1. Mix beef, coriander, garlic, cloves, ginger, cumin, salt, in a large bowl. Make a well in the center of the beef, add beaten egg, beat beef into the egg. Roll beef, 1 tablespoon at a time between the palms to form balls. Prepare and measure remaining ingredients. Mix saffron into water in a small cup. Place meat balls and all other ingredients handy to the stove in the order listed.

2. Set *wok* over medium heat for 30 seconds, swirl in oil, melt butter. Add onions and stir-fry golden brown 3 to 5 minutes. Add tomato paste, yogurt, and cardamom seeds; bring to simmer. Turn heat to low, add meat balls and 1 cup water, stir once, cover, simmer 20 minutes. Add saffron and water mixture, cook another 5 minutes. Serve hot.

Serves 6.

GINGER BEEF

This is distinctly different, and ginger fans love it.

3 tablespoons oil
1 pound beef steak

⅓ cup thinly sliced ginger
2 tablespoons oyster sauce

1. Measure oil. Slice steak into pieces 2 inches long by 1 inch wide by ¼ inch thick. Measure ginger and oyster sauce. Set by the stove in order listed.
2. Set *wok* over high heat for 30 seconds; swirl in oil; heat to almost smoking; add beef and stir-fry 1 minute. Add ginger, and stir-fry 4 minutes. Add oyster sauce and stir-fry 2 minutes more. Serve at once.

Serves 4, more if other dishes are offered.

CALCUTTA BEEF CURRY

An easy beef curry to serve with rice, Raita, Hot Mango Chutney, and Onion Sambal. Use light cream instead of coconut milk if you prefer.

1 pound bottom round
2 cups boiling water
¼ cup grated coconut
½ cup boiling water
1 tablespoon ground
  coriander
½ teaspoon turmeric
½ teaspoon ground cumin

½ teaspoon red pepper
  flakes
⅛ teaspoon ground ginger
¼ cup oil
1 large onion chopped
4 tablespoons lemon juice,
  strained

1. Cut meat into 1-inch cubes, cover with boiling water and simmer until tender, about 40 minutes. Cover grated coconut with boiling water and let soak while meat cooks. Strain out

coconut, measure ¼ cup coconut milk, and mix into it the coriander, turmeric, cumin, red pepper and ginger.

2. Set *wok* over medium heat for 30 seconds, add oil, count to 20, add onion, and stir-fry until golden, 3 to 5 minutes. Mix in paste of coconut milk and spices, and simmer 5 minutes, stirring. Lift meat cubes with slotted spoon from stock it cooked in, add to onions with remaining coconut milk. Add enough beef stock so meat cooks almost immersed in sauce. Simmer 10 minutes more. Add half the lemon juice, cook 5 minutes more. Add as much more lemon juice as you can enjoy. Keep warm until served.

Serves 4.

Chicken

CHICKEN WITH TIGER LILIES

Dried tiger lily buds are available at Oriental specialty food shops. To me, they have a faintly pineapple flavor, and combine well with chicken in this recipe.

1½ cups tiger lily buds	3 tablespoons chicken fat,
4 chicken breasts	or oil
2 slices fresh ginger, ¼ inch thick	2 tablespoons soy sauce
	Water

1. Cover lily buds with boiling water and soak 15 minutes. Bone chicken (2 whole breasts or 4 halves), and cut into pieces 2 inches long by ½ inch wide and ½ inch thick. Sliver ginger. Measure fat, soy sauce, and place about ½ cup of water with all other ingredients by the stove. Drain lilies, squeeze dry.

2. Set *wok* over high heat for 30 seconds, swirl in fat, count to 20. Add ginger; stir-fry ½ minute. Add chicken and stir-fry until browned lightly. Add soy sauce; stir-fry until chicken

feels tender. Add lilies; reduce heat to medium, cover, and cook 8 to 10 minutes. As liquids in *wok* reduce, you'll hear a sizzling. Add a little water so ingredients cook in enough sauce to keep them from drying out or burning. Keep warm until ready to serve.

Serves 4 to 6, more if other dishes are offered.

CHICKEN STIR-FRIED WITH WALNUTS

Luscious chunks of chicken and lots of crunchy walnuts. One of our top favorites. For the family, serve with Braised Pumpkin and a side dish of Sweet-and-Sour Sauce; for company, serve with Shrimps Sweet-and-Sour, and rice . . . Celery Stir-fried with Mushrooms, too, if you can manage. Takes about 25 minutes to prepare. Freeze chicken skin and bones to make soup.

4 tablespoons oil	1½ tablespoons cornstarch
1½ cups whole walnut meats	½ teaspoon salt
2 slices ginger ⅛ inch thick, or ½ teaspoon ground	1 tablespoon dry sherry
	1 tablespoon sugar
	2 tablespoons soy sauce
2 cloves garlic, peeled, sliced	1 teaspoon cornstarch
3 pounds chicken	½ cup Chicken Stock or water
1 egg white	

1. Measure oil, walnut meats; prepare ginger, garlic. Bone and skin chicken and cut into 1-inch cubes (more or less). Mix chicken with unbeaten egg white, then toss in 1½ tablespoons cornstarch mixed with salt. Measure sherry, sugar, and soy sauce. Mix 1 teaspoon cornstarch with Chicken Stock. Set ingredients by stove in order listed along with a slotted spoon and a small bowl.

2. Set *wok* over high heat for 30 seconds, swirl in oil, count to 20. Add walnuts and quickly stir-fry 3 minutes.

Don't let walnuts darken or they will be bitter. Remove with slotted spoon to bowl. At once add ginger and garlic to the *wok;* stir once or twice. Add chicken; stir-fry until blanched on all sides, about 2 minutes. Add sherry; toss. Add sugar and soy sauce, turn heat to medium, and stir-fry 3 minutes more. Push chicken to one side. Stir up cornstarch mixture; pour down side of *wok;* stir until sauce thickens and clears. Stir in chicken and walnuts, and serve at once if possible.

Serves 4 to 5, more if other dishes are offered.

CHICKEN AND TOMATOES STIR-FRIED, VIETNAM

To give this the authentic flavor, you will need *Nuoc Mam,* the Vietnamese fish sauce, but it is good made with Chinese fish sauce, oyster sauce, or plain soy sauce.

3 tablespoons oil
1½ pounds cut-up chicken
1 large shallot, minced, or
  1 tablespoon minced
  onion
¼ teaspoon pepper
1 teaspoon salt
2 cloves garlic, peeled,
  crushed

2 large tomatoes, chopped
1 large shallot, minced, or
  1 tablespoon minced
  onion
1 tablespoon tomato paste
1 tablespoon *Nuoc Mam,*
  or fish sauce

1. Measure oil. Let chicken pieces stand 1 hour in mixture of shallot, pepper, and salt. Measure and prepare all other ingredients and set by stove in order listed.

2. Set *wok* over high heat for 30 seconds, swirl in oil, count to 30, and add chicken pieces. Toss once, lower heat to medium, stir-fry 5 minutes more. Cover; simmer 10 minutes. Add garlic; stir-fry 30 seconds. Add tomatoes, shallot, and tomato paste. Mix and stir until tomato renders its juice; cover, cook another 5 minutes. Add fish sauce; stir-fry another

2 minutes. If dish is dry, add a tablespoon or two of water. Keep warm until ready to serve.

Serves 4, more if other dishes are offered.

CHICKEN AND VEGETABLES, SWEET AND SOUR

A complete meal for about 4, with rice; for 6, batter-dipped deep-fried shrimp or with pork.

3 tablespoons oil
2 chicken breasts (4 halves)
1 egg white, unbeaten
1½ tablespoons cornstarch
½ teaspoon salt
1 cup Chinese cabbage, shredded (optional)
3 medium stalks celery, shredded
8 water chestnuts, rinsed, diced
½ cup bamboo shoots, rinsed, shredded

1 cup pineapple tidbits, drained
½ to ⅔ cup pineapple syrup
1 tablespoon light brown sugar
½ teaspoon salt
⅛ teaspoon pepper
2 tablespoons vinegar
1 cup water
3 tablespoons cornstarch
3 tablespoons water

1. Measure oil. Bone and skin chicken, cut into pieces 1 to 2 inches long by ½ inch wide by ¼ inch thick, more or less. Mix with egg white, and toss with cornstarch and salt. Wash and cut cabbage, celery, water chestnuts, and bamboo shoots. Drain and measure pineapple, reserving syrup. In a small bowl mix pineapple syrup with sugar, salt, pepper, vinegar, water. Mix cornstarch with water in a cup. Place all ingredients by the stove in the order listed.

2. Set *wok* over high heat for 30 seconds, swirl in oil, count to 30, add chicken and stir-fry until blanched, about 2 minutes. Add vegetables, cabbage, celery, water chestnuts, bamboo shoots, pineapple, tossing quickly until well mixed after each addition. Pour pineapple syrup mixture down side

of *wok;* stir until it simmers. Push solid ingredients to one side of *wok,* pour cornstarch mixture down *wok* side and stir until sauce thickens and clears. Mix all ingredients, and serve when dinner is ready.

Serves 4 to 6, more if other dishes are offered.

CHICKEN CHUNKS
WITH MUSHROOMS AND SNOW PEAS

Everyone likes this Chinese dish. Once the ingredients are prepared, it cooks in about 20 minutes.

2 tablespoons oil	4 ounces water chestnuts
2 pounds chicken thighs	¼ pound fresh snow peas,
1 tablespoon soy sauce	or 1 package frozen
5 slices ginger, ¼ inch	¼ teaspoon pepper
thick	½ teaspoon sugar
1 teaspoon salt	1 tablespoon oyster sauce
2 cups water	(or omit)
15 Chinese dried mushrooms	2 tablespoons cornstarch
2 scallions	3 tablespoons water

1. Measure oil. Chop chicken thighs into thirds, removing bone. Rinse to wash away any broken bits of bone, and toss in soy sauce. Slice ginger. Measure salt. Bring 2 cups water to a boil. Cover mushrooms, soak 20 minutes; drain, reserving liquid. Chop scallions into 1-inch lengths. Rinse drained water chestnuts. String snow peas, cover with boiling water and simmer until half tender, or thaw frozen snow peas. Measure pepper, sugar, oyster sauce. Mix cornstarch with water. Place prepared ingredients by the stove in the order listed.

2. Set *wok* over high heat for 30 seconds, swirl in oil, count to 20, add chicken pieces and stir-fry 2 minutes. Add ginger and salt; stir-fry 1 minute. Add mushroom water, mushrooms, scallions, water chestnuts, snow peas, pepper, and sugar; cover, simmer 10 minutes, or until chicken is tender.

Stir in oyster sauce; bring to a simmer. Pour cornstarch mixture down side of *wok,* stir until sauce thickens and clears. Serve as soon as possible.

Serves 6, more if other dishes are offered.

CHICKEN VELVET WITH VEGETABLES

A classic of Chinese cooking, made by pounding chicken to a pulp with water and cornstarch and deep-frying in oil. This variation is made in a blender, much easier than pounding, and includes vegetables.

1 chicken breast (2 halves)	½ cup chopped fresh
1 cup Chicken Stock	mushrooms
1 teaspoon dry sherry	¼ pound fresh snow peas,
1 teaspoon salt	or 1 package frozen
¼ teaspoon pepper	½ cup celery in rounds ¼
1 tablespoon cornstarch	inch thick
3 egg whites, beaten stiff	½ cup Chicken Stock
2 cups oil	1 teaspoon dry sherry, or
2 slices ginger ¼ inch	soy sauce
thick, or ¼ teaspoon	½ teaspoon salt
ground ginger	1 tablespoon cornstarch
¼ cup skinned whole	
almonds	

1. Skin and bone chicken (save to make Chicken Stock). Cube meat and place in blender at high speed 1 minute. With blender on low, add Chicken Stock, sherry, salt, pepper, and cornstarch. Remove to bowl and fold in egg whites.

2. Measure oil, ginger, almonds, and prepare mushrooms. String fresh snow peas, cover with boiling water, cook until half tender, and drain; or thaw and dry frozen peas. Slice celery. Mix Chicken Stock with sherry, salt, and cornstarch. Place ingredients by the stove in order listed with a sieve or slotted spoon. Warm medium serving bowl in oven.

3. Set *wok* over high heat 30 seconds, swirl in oil, heat to about 300°. Add chicken mixture, 1 tablespoon at a time, and fry only until white. Keep warm in oven. Remove all but 4 tablespoons oil. Add ginger, almonds, mushrooms, and stir-fry 1 minute. Add snow peas and celery; stir-fry until dark green. Pour stock and cornstarch mixture down side of *wok*; stir until thick and clear, pour over chicken cakes, and serve at once.

Serves 4 to 6, more if other dishes are offered.

FRIED CHICKEN, JAPAN

Chicken wings seasoned the Japanese way and fried quickly in oil. Crush minced fresh ginger in a garlic crusher to get ginger juice. Use as part of a Japanese meal or as an appetizer.

1 pound chicken wings	2 teaspoons ginger juice
2 tablespoons Japanese soy sauce	Cornstarch
3 tablespoons dry sherry	3 cups oil

1. Cut wings apart at the joint and chop off wing tips (freeze to make Chicken Stock). Marinate wings in soy sauce, sherry, and ginger juice, mixed in a medium bowl, for 1 hour. Toss occasionally. Half fill a small bowl with cornstarch, and dredge wings. Place by the stove with a Chinese sieve or a slotted spoon. Set a serving dish in the oven at 250°, and line it with paper towel.

2. Set *wok* over high heat for 30 seconds, add oil, heat to 350° or until a day-old cube of bread sizzles when it hits oil. Fry wings in 2 or 3 batches, until golden brown, 4 to 5 minutes.

Serves 2 to 4, more if offered as an appetizer.

CHICKEN PULAO WITH SHRIMP, INDIA

Exotic and easy on the hostess. Serve with hot bread and tossed salad. Best made in an enameled heavy skillet that has a heavy lid, or in a large casserole.

1 teaspoon oil
2 sticks butter
2 large onions, sliced
1 pound cut-up chicken
1 teaspoon salt
3 cloves garlic, peeled, minced
3 tablespoons dark seedless raisins
¼ teaspoon cinnamon
⅛ teaspoon peeled cardamom, ground
⅛ teaspoon mace

1 teaspoon ground cloves
⅛ teaspoon pepper
2 cups raw converted rice
1 pound raw shrimp, shelled, deveined
2 cups Chicken Stock
2 cups Beef Stock or consommé
½ teaspoon saffron
1 tablespoon water
2 tablespoons whole almonds

1. Measure oil and butter; prepare onions; cut chicken in pieces of similar size. Measure salt. Into a small bowl measure garlic, raisins, cinnamon, cardamom, mace, cloves, pepper. Wash rice. Prepare shrimp. Measure Chicken Stock and Beef Stock. Soak saffron in water. Measure almonds. Set ingredients by stove in order listed.

2. In skillet or casserole, warm oil over medium heat, melt butter, and stir-fry onions until crisp. Remove and reserve. Add chicken pieces and stir-fry with salt 1 minute. Add mixed spices, and stir-fry until chicken is browning, 5 to 6 minutes. Add rice; stir-fry 5 minutes or until opaque-looking. Add shrimp, mix well, add Chicken and Beef Stocks, stir until boiling, cover, reduce heat to minimum, simmer until water is absorbed, about 20 minutes. Stir in saffron mixture and al-

monds 5 minutes before rice is tender. Serve hot, sprinkled with crisped onions.

Serves 6.

CHICKEN AND FRUIT CURRY, JAVA

Glamorous fare rich with the flavor of fruit and freshly ground spice. We like it with crisp batter-dipped shrimp and plain boiled rice. You need two cups cooked chicken, preferably white meat.

1½ tablespoons oil
¼ cup tomato juice
1 tablespoon lemon juice
1 small onion, minced
1 clove garlic, peeled, minced
½ tablespoon ground coriander
1 teaspoon turmeric
1 teaspoon ground cumin
⅛ teaspoon chili powder
½ teaspoon dry mustard

¼ teaspoon ground fennel
¼ teaspoon pepper
4 tablespoons white vinegar
½ cup sliced canned mangoes and syrup
¼ cup pineapple chunks and syrup
½ banana, peeled, sliced
1 tablespoon honey
1 teaspoon salt
2 cups cooked chicken cubes

1. Measure and prepare ingredients and set by the stove.

2. Set *wok* over medium heat 20 seconds, swirl in oil, stir in tomato and lemon juice and all other ingredients except chicken. Mix, lower heat, simmer 15 minutes, covered. Ladle out 1 cupful and set aside. Add chicken to the *wok*, heat through, stirring, then serve with the reserved extra sauce, hot, in a side dish.

Serves 4 to 6.

CHICKEN WITH FRUIT AND ALMONDS, MALAYSIA

An aromatic curry that is one of our favorites. Increase chili if you like hot curries. Nice with rice, a deep-fried batter-dipped fish, and a good chutney. A good patio meal.

2 cups milk
1 cup grated coconut
1 teaspoon oil
3 tablespoons butter
3 medium onions
1 tablespoon ground coriander
1 teaspoon ground anise
½ teaspoon saffron
1 teaspoon ground ginger
¼ teaspoon chili powder
2 cloves garlic, peeled, minced

2 tablespoons grated lemon rind
3 tablespoons lemon juice
2 tablespoons damson preserve, or plum jam
1 teaspoon sugar
1 teaspoon salt
3 pounds chicken
1 cup peeled whole almonds
6 cups cooked rice
Chutney

1. Bring milk to a boil, add coconut, turn off heat, and soak 30 minutes. Drain, reserving liquid. Squeeze coconut dry and reserve also.

2. Measure oil and butter. Slice onions into rings, place in a medium bowl, and toss with coriander, anise, saffron, ginger, chili, garlic, grated rind, lemon juice, preserve, sugar, and salt. Skin and bone chicken, cut into 1-inch cubes. Measure almonds. Place rice in serving dish and keep warm, and gather all other ingredients by the stove.

3. Set *wok* over medium heat for 30 seconds, swirl in oil, melt butter, add coconut shreds, stir-fry until lightly browned. Remove to onion and spice mixture, toss. Add chicken to the *wok*, toss to coat with butter. Add onion mixture and toss. Add coconut milk and almonds. Bring to a rapid boil, lower

heat, and simmer 10 minutes or until chicken is tender and sauce is thick. Serve with rice and chutney.

Serves 6, more if other dishes are offered.

Other Meats

LAMB STRIPS AND LIMA BEANS

A favorite with Chinese meals. Takes about 15 minutes to prepare and cook. Good without the limas on toasted English muffins for a Sunday night supper or an after-ski snack. Have 1 pound cut from the next leg of lamb you buy, and freeze it to have handy for Lamb Strips.

2 tablespoons oil
3 cloves garlic, peeled
1 pound from leg of lamb
2 teaspoons soy sauce

1 tablespoon oil
½ package frozen lima beans
1 teaspoon soy sauce

1. Measure oil, crush garlic, slice lamb into strips 2 inches by 1 inch by ⅛ inch. (Easiest to do when lamb is slightly frozen.) Measure soy and 1 tablespoon oil. Thaw and dry limas. Measure another teaspoon soy. Set ingredients by the stove in the order listed, and warm the serving dish.

2. Set *wok* over high heat for 30 seconds, swirl in 2 tablespoons oil, count to 30, add crushed garlic and stir until browning. Turn heat to medium, add lamb and 2 teaspoons soy sauce, and stir-fry 3 minutes. Turn lamb into serving dish, pour gravy over it. Turn heat under *wok* to medium high, add 1 tablespoon oil, count to 20, add lima beans, stir-fry 2 minutes. Add 1 teaspoon soy sauce, stir-fry 1 minute more, pour limas over lamb strips, and serve at once.

Serves 2 to 4, more if other dishes are offered.

LAMB KORMA, INDIA

Tender lamb chunks in a creamy aromatic curry-flavored sauce, ready in about 45 minutes. Serve with boiled rice, chutney, Raita, or Onion Samball. A family favorite.

1 tablespoon oil	1 tablespoon ground cumin
3 tablespoons butter	2 cardamom seeds, peeled
1 large onion	½ teaspoon ground ginger
1 clove garlic, peeled	6 whole cloves
1 pound of leg of lamb	¼ teaspoon red pepper
½ teaspoon salt	flakes
1 pint plain yogurt	1 8-ounce can tomato sauce
1 tablespoon ground	
coriander	

1. Measure oil and butter. Slice onion, mince garlic. Cut lamb into 1-inch cubes; marinate with salt and yogurt for 15 minutes. Grind coriander and cumin, peel cardamom seeds, measure ginger, cloves, and red pepper flakes, and mix into tomato sauce. Set all ingredients by stove in order listed.

2. Set *wok* over medium heat for 30 seconds, swirl in oil, melt butter, add onion and garlic, and stir-fry until onion is golden, 3 to 5 minutes. Add lamb and yogurt, and tomato sauce with spices. Stir well, cover, simmer until meat is tender, 20 to 30 minutes. Remove cover last few minutes of cooking so sauce is well thickened.

Serves about 4, more if other dishes are offered.

KIDNEY STIR-FRIED WITH ONION
AND MUSHROOMS

Super, when kidney is very fresh. Lamb kidneys are best. Serve with boiled rice and a stir-fried or Western-style green vegetable. Remove kidney in slanted slices ¼ inch thick from membrane, soak overnight in ice water in refrigerator before using.

4 tablespoons chicken fat or oil	¼ teaspoon black pepper
1 large onion, blender-chopped	2 tablespoons dry sherry
½ pound fresh mushrooms, chopped	1 tablespoon soy sauce
	1½ tablespoons cornstarch
1 pound beef or lamb kidneys, sliced, soaked, drained	½ cup Chicken Stock or Beef Stock
	½ cup finely minced parsley
	Salt to taste

1. Measure fat, chop onion, slice mushrooms into lengths ⅛ inch thick. Marinate kidney slices in pepper, sherry, and soy sauce briefly. Mix cornstarch with stock. Mince parsley. Place all ingredients by the stove in order listed with a slotted spoon and a small bowl.

2. Set *wok* over high heat for 30 seconds, swirl in 2 tablespoons fat, count to 30, add onion, and stir-fry until translucent, 3 to 4 minutes. Remove to bowl, leaving as much fat as possible in *wok*. Add 1 tablespoon more fat and stir-fry mushrooms until wilted, about 2 minutes. Remove to bowl. Add 1 tablespoon fat to *wok*, heat until almost smoking, and stir-fry kidney slices 2 to 3 minutes. Add stock and cornstarch mixture, stir until gravy forms, return onion and mushrooms to *wok*, lower heat, simmer covered about 6 minutes. Add salt to taste, turn into serving dish, and sprinkle all over with finely minced parsley.

Serves 2 to 3, more if other dishes are offered.

LAMB KIDNEY, INDIA

Any very fresh kidney is delicious if meat is cut away from all membrane (a tedious procedure), and then soaked several hours or overnight in ice water in refrigerator. I think so, anyway. This Indian dish is particularly savory.

1 teaspoon oil
4 tablespoons butter
1 medium onion, chopped
3 cloves garlic, peeled, minced
1 teaspoon minced ginger, or ½ teaspoon ground
1 teaspoon turmeric
1½ teaspoons ground cumin
1 cardamom seed, peeled
1½ teaspoons ground coriander
5 whole cloves
½ pint yogurt
1 tablespoon tomato paste
1 cup hot water
6 lamb kidneys, sliced, soaked overnight in ice water, drained
Salt to taste

1. Measure and prepare ingredients and set by stove in order listed.
2. Set *wok* over medium-high heat for 30 seconds, swirl in oil, add butter. When it melts, add onion; stir-fry until golden, 3 to 5 minutes. Add garlic, ginger, turmeric, cumin, cardamom seed, coriander, cloves, and stir-fry 5 minutes more. Stir in yogurt, tomato paste, water; heat to simmer, and cook 5 minutes. Add kidney pieces, and when sauce simmers again, cover and cook over lowered heat 30 minutes. Remove cover last few minutes to further thicken sauce. Keep warm until ready to serve.

Serves 6, more if other dishes are offered.

GIBLETS, VIETNAM

Save up chicken hearts and gizzards in the freezer, and when you have 2 cups try this recipe. Serve with rice and a crispy vegetable.

2 tablespoons oil	⅛ teaspoon ground ginger
2 large shallots, minced, or 2 tablespoons minced onion	¼ teaspoon pepper
	½ teaspoon salt
	1 tablespoon *Nuoc Mam,*
2 cups chicken hearts and gizzards	or oyster sauce, or fish sauce
¼ pound fresh mushrooms	1½ cups cauliflower florets
12 dried Chinese mushrooms	1 tablespoon cornstarch

1. Measure oil. Peel and mince shallots. Slice giblets into pieces ⅛ inch thick. Wipe fresh mushrooms; slice into lengths ¼ inch thick. Cover dried mushrooms with 1 cup boiling water, soak 20 minutes, drain, reserving ⅔ cup water. Sliver dried mushrooms. Measure ginger, pepper, salt, *Nuoc Mam.* Cut cauliflower into tiniest florets, cover with boiling water, bring back to a boil, simmer 3 minutes, and drain well. Mix cornstarch with reserved mushroom water. Place all ingredients by the stove in order listed.

2. Set *wok* over medium heat for 30 seconds, swirl in oil, count to 30, add shallots, mix once, add giblets, mix well. Add all mushrooms, and stir-fry 1 minute. Add ginger, pepper, salt, and *Nuoc Mam,* and simmer 5 minutes. Add blanched cauliflower, mix well, cover and cook another 3 minutes. Push ingredients to one side, dribble cornstarch mixture down side of *wok,* stir until it thickens and clears. Mix all ingredients, and serve at once.

Serves 4, more if other dishes are offered.

CHICKEN LIVERS AND GREEN APPLES

Flavorful adjunct to any Oriental meal, and a nice appetizer, too.

¼ cup oil
1 medium onion, chopped
1 pound chicken livers
2 tablespoons dry sherry
4 hard-boiled eggs
2 medium-large apples, tart
1 tablespoon lemon juice

¼ teaspoon ground coriander
⅛ teaspoon ground cumin
⅛ teaspoon ground turmeric
⅛ teaspoon ground ginger
½ teaspoon salt
¼ teaspoon pepper

1. Measure oil. Blender-chop onion. Wash livers; dry on paper towel; quarter. Measure sherry. Shell and chop eggs. Core and peel apples, cut into chunks and blender-chop. Strain lemon juice, grind and/or measure spices, salt, and pepper. Arrange by stove in order listed.

2. Set *wok* over medium-high heat for 30 seconds, swirl in oil, count to 20, add onion. Stir-fry until golden, 3 to 5 minutes. Add chicken livers, toss to coat with oil. Add sherry, chopped egg, and apple, mix well. Sprinkle with lemon juice, coriander, cumin, turmeric, ginger, salt, and pepper. Stir-fry 2 to 3 minutes, until juices no longer run red from liver, and keep warm until ready to serve. Can be served cold, too.

Serves 4, more as an appetizer.

CHICKEN LIVERS AND GIZZARDS DEEP-FRIED

Deep-fried to serve as a crispy dish with a Chinese meal, or can be offered as appetizers. Chicken parts should be very fresh.

½ to 1 cup chicken livers
½ to 1 cup gizzards
2 tablespoons soy sauce
2 tablespoons dry sherry

Flour or cornstarch
3 cups oil
Salt and pepper to taste

1. Wash livers and gizzards, drain, dry on paper towel. Divide livers at joining place and make a long gash in each piece. Divide gizzards at joining place, and make 3 gashes in each piece. Marinate both in mixture of soy sauce and sherry 15 minutes. Drain, dredge with flour or cornstarch, and place by the stove with a Chinese sieve or slotted spoon, the oil, salt, and pepper. Place serving dish lined with paper towel in 250° oven.

2. Set *wok* over high heat for 30 seconds, add oil, heat to 350° or until a bit of dry bread sizzles when hits oil. Add one quarter of the giblets and fry to medium brown, 2 to 3 minutes. Scoop out with sieve, drain and keep warm in oven. Repeat for remaining three batches, sprinkle all with salt and pepper and serve at once.

Serves 4 to 6, more as an appetizer.

DUCK WITH PINEAPPLE AND MUSHROOMS

A wonderful way with this bird and a dish to feature, though it takes time to prepare. Omit Chinese mushrooms if you don't care for them.

3- to 4-pound duck
12 dried Chinese
  mushrooms
1 can pineapple slices,
  drained
½ to ⅔ cup pineapple
  syrup

Salt to taste
2 tablespoons oil
2 tablespoons soy sauce
1 tablespoon dry sherry
½ cup water
2 tablespoons light brown
  sugar

1. Set oven at 350°. Place duck in uncovered roasting pan and roast about 1 hour, or until almost done. Remove, turn off oven, cool duck. Soak dried mushrooms in boiling water for 20 minutes, then drain. When duck is cool, remove skin. Cut meat from bones in slices 1 inch long by 1 inch wide by about ½ inch thick. Discard carcass. Arrange meat in ovenproof serving dish, with Chinese mushrooms and pineapple slices, quartered. Place pineapple syrup, salt (I use about 1 teaspoon), oil, soy sauce, sherry, water, and sugar in a small saucepan.

2. About 1½ hours before dinner, heat oven to 350°. Bring pineapple syrup mixture to simmer, pour over duck casserole, place in heated oven, covered loosely so steam can escape, and bake about 1 hour.

Serves 4 to 6.

10. Vegetables and Garnishes

IN ORIENTAL MEALS vegetables are as important as, and often a part of, the main meat or fish dishes. One of the best things about Chinese cooking is the texture of the vegetables. Most people do not realize that the vegetables they eat in Chinese restaurants are the ones they eat at home. The difference is in the cutting and cooking.

Carrots, turnips, green beans, celery, turn up in Chinese food as frequently as foreign fare such as snow peas, bean sprouts, and the wonderful dried Chinese mushrooms. Flash-cooked, they not only look and taste more interesting, but also keep their nutritive contents intact. Whatever isn't sealed in by searing is captured in the glazed juices served with them. If you leave vegetables unpeeled—and in most Chinese recipes you can—they'll retain even more of their nutritional content.

Though cooking times for each vegetable are given in the recipes, the most accurate timer is your own eye. Vegetables become tender in more or less time, depending upon their freshness, the heat of the pan, and other factors. At high heats, they generally loose some opaqueness (onions are a clear example) in 1 minute, and begin to brighten in color. After 2 to 3 minutes a bright green turns to a dark intense green which will yellow as the vegetable becomes overdone. A recipe can suggest when this will happen—and I often use a timer when following Oriental recipes. But only you can see what is occurring with a given batch of green beans. Vegetables should be removed a shade underdone, while color is still intense. They will continue to cook in their own heat and will be just right when served.

Vegetable Dishes

CHINESE MUSHROOMS, SNOW PEAS, AND BAMBOO SHOOTS

This is a meaty vegetable dish, distinctly different, delicious. The mushrooms alone are good, too.

2 cups dried Chinese
 mushrooms
1 teaspoon soy sauce
½ teaspoon salt
1 teaspoon sugar
1 teaspoon cornstarch
2 tablespoons oil
2 scallions, in 1-inch shreds
1 slice ginger, ½ inch thick,
 minced very fine
½ cup Chicken Stock

½ cup mushroom water
4 tablespoons oyster sauce
1 teaspoon cornstarch
2 tablespoons water
1 tablespoon oil
4 ounces snow peas, strung,
 parboiled, or 1 package
 frozen or flat Italian
 beans
1 can bamboo shoots, rinsed
1 teaspoon salt

1. Cover mushrooms with boiling water, soak 20 minutes. Drain, reserving ½ cup liquid. Sprinkle mushrooms with soy sauce, salt, sugar, cornstarch, and mix well. Set by stove with remaining ingredients in order listed. Place serving platter in oven at 250°.

2. Set *wok* over high heat for 30 seconds, swirl in oil, count to 30, add mushrooms, stir-fry 2 minutes. Lower heat to medium, add scallions, ginger; stir-fry 5 minutes. Add Chicken Stock, mushroom water; cover, simmer 15 minutes. Add oyster

sauce; stir well. Add cornstarch mixed with water, and simmer until sauce thickens and clears. Pour into medium bowl and keep warm.

3. Turn heat to medium high, add 1 tablespoon oil, count to 20, add snow peas and bamboo shoots. Sprinkle with salt, stir-fry 3 minutes. Dish into serving platter, pour mushrooms over snow peas, and serve soon.

Serves 4 to 6, more if other dishes are offered.

GREEN CABBAGE WITH CRABMEAT SAUCE

Green and white, and delicately flavored. With rice, it makes a complete meal for two persons. I use Alaska King crab for this dish.

2 small celery cabbages	1 teaspoon sherry
½ teaspoon baking soda	1 cup Chicken Stock
2 tablespoons oil	¼ teaspoon black pepper
1 teaspoon salt	1 teaspoon soy sauce
2 tablespoons oil	1 tablespoon cornstarch
6 ounces raw crabmeat	½ cup Chicken Stock

1. Cut washed celery cabbages into 6 lengths each. Cover with boiling water, add soda, and soak 2 minutes. Drain well. Measure remaining ingredients, and place by stove in order listed, mixing cornstarch with ½ cup Chicken Stock. Place serving platter in oven at 150°.

2. Set *wok* over high heat for 30 seconds, swirl in oil, count to 20, add cabbage, and toss with oil using two spatulas, until cabbage turns brighter green and leaves begin to wilt, 2 to 3 minutes. Season with salt, and remove to serving platter. Swirl 2 tablespoons oil into *wok*, add crab, stir-fry 1 minute gently to avoid breaking. Add sherry, Chicken Stock, pepper, soy sauce, and simmer 2 minutes. Pour cornstarch mixture down

side of *wok,* and stir gently until sauce thickens and clears. Pour over vegetables and serve at once. Offer soy sauce at the table.

Serves 2 or 3, more if other dishes are offered.

CHINESE VEGETABLES AND LOBSTER SAUCE

Wonderful texture and flavor—crunchy, delicate, and just delicious. The lobster is a background rather than an up-front ingredient. I use 1 package of frozen South African rock lobster tails for this. Takes 10 minutes to cook, about 30 to prepare. Serve with rice.

1 tablespoon oil	7 ounces raw lobster tails
1 teaspoon salt	¼ cup roasted almonds
1 clove garlic, peeled, smashed	1½ tablespoons soy sauce
8 dried Chinese mushrooms	1 tablespoon oyster sauce
8 fresh mushrooms	2 tablespoons dry sherry
½ cup Chinese cabbage, shredded, or celery	1 slice ginger, ⅛ inch thick
½ cup blender-chopped onion	½ cup Chicken Stock
½ cup diced bamboo shoots	1 tablespoon cornstarch
	2 teaspoons sugar
	¼ cup mushroom liquid

1. Measure oil, salt, and prepare garlic. Pour ½ cup boiling water over Chinese mushrooms, soak 20 minutes, drain, reserving liquid. Wipe fresh mushrooms, slice into lengths ⅛ inch thick. Shred or chop cabbage, onion, bamboo shoots, cut lobster tails into slices ⅛ inch thick across the grain. Measure all other ingredients, mixing cornstarch with sugar and mushroom liquid, and place by the stove in order listed.

2. Set *wok* over high heat 30 seconds, swirl in oil, count to 30, add salt and garlic. Stir-fry until garlic turns golden.

Add both kinds of mushrooms; stir-fry 30 seconds. Add cabbage, onion, bamboo shoots, and stir-fry ½ minute after each addition. Add lobster slices; stir-fry 2 minutes more. Add almonds, soy and oyster sauce, sherry, and ginger; mix well. Add Chicken Stock; mix until it simmers. Add cornstarch mixture; stir until sauce thickens and clears. Taste, add more oyster sauce if you like. Keep warm until ready to serve.

Serves 4 to 6, more if other dishes are offered.

VEGETABLE MIX, VIETNAM

A crunchy vegetable combination to serve for a multiple-dish dinner. *Nuoc Mam* sauce is available at many Oriental food shops.

4 tablespoons oil
1 cup cauliflower florets
1 cup shredded carrots
1 cup shredded turnips
2 celery stalks, diced
2 medium leeks, cleaned, in shreds, or 1 small onion

2 tablespoons *Nuoc Mam* sauce, or fish, oyster, or soy sauce
¼ teaspoon Five Spice Powder, or ground anise, clove, pepper

1. Measure oil, break cauliflower into tiny florets, and shred carrots and turnip on coarse side of grater. Prepare celery, leeks, measure *Nuoc Mam*, and Spice Powder. Set ingredients by stove in order listed.

2. Set *wok* over high heat for 30 seconds, swirl in oil, count to 30. Add vegetables in order listed, tossing in oil after each addition—cauliflower, carrots, turnips, celery, leeks. Stir-fry a total of 5 minutes, then mix in *Nuoc Mam* sauce and Spice Powder. Toss ½ minute; serve as soon as possible.

Serves 6, more if other dishes are offered.

VEGETABLE CURRY, INDIA

Serve with boiled rice and a meat kebab, or with broiled meats Western-style.

1 teaspoon oil
2 tablespoons butter
2 medium onions, sliced
1 slice ginger, ⅛ inch thick, minced, or ¼ teaspoon ground
1 teaspoon ground thyme
1 teaspoon ground marjoram
1 teaspoon minced parsley
1 teaspoon basil
1 teaspoon dill

2 bay leaves, crumbled
1 teaspoon turmeric
½ tablespoon salt
1 pound mushrooms, halved
6 small potatoes, peeled, quartered
3 tomatoes, in thick slices
1 tablespoon lemon juice, strained
2 teaspoons curry powder

1. Gather prepared ingredients by stove in order listed.

2. Set *wok* over medium heat for 30 seconds, swirl in oil, add butter. Turn onions into melted butter; add ginger, thyme, marjoram, parsley, basil, dill, bay leaves, turmeric, and salt. Stir-fry until golden, 4 to 5 minutes. Add mushrooms; stir-fry 4 to 5 minutes. Add potatoes; stir-fry 3 minutes. Add tomatoes, mix well, cook uncovered 25 to 30 minutes, or until potatoes are tender. About 5 minutes before they are ready, add lemon juice and curry. Keep warm until ready to serve.

Serves 4 to 6, more if served at a multi-dish dinner.

SPINACH AND MUSHROOMS

A strongly flavored, meaty vegetable dish, good with broiled and grilled meats, and especially with liver. Quickly prepared, and cooks in minutes.

3 tablespoons oil
2 cloves garlic, peeled, smashed
1 cup mushrooms in lengths ⅛ inch thick

½ teaspoon salt
1 pound washed leaf spinach
1 teaspoon sugar
Soy sauce

1. Prepare ingredients and set by stove in order listed.

2. Set *wok* over high heat for 30 seconds, swirl in oil, count to 30, add garlic and stir until lightly browned. Add mushrooms and salt; stir-fry until mushrooms wilt, 2 to 3 minutes. Add spinach and sugar; stir-fry until spinach softens and is intense green. Serve at once, and offer soy sauce at the table.

Serves 4, more if other dishes are offered.

CELERY STIR-FRIED WITH FRESH MUSHROOMS

Fast and easy, particularly good with beef dishes and steak Western-style—a family favorite, with meaty flavor and lots of crunch.

2 tablespoons oil
½ pound fresh mushrooms
2 tablespoons soy sauce

½ teaspoon salt
1 teaspoon sugar
1 medium bunch of celery

1. Measure oil. Wipe mushrooms and cut into lengths ¼ inch thick. Measure soy sauce, salt, sugar. Remove celery leaves, wash stems, then roll-cut in 1-inch diagonals. Assemble all ingredients by the stove in the order listed.

2. Set *wok* over high heat for 30 seconds, swirl in oil, count to 20, add mushroom slices, stir-fry 1 minute. Add soy sauce, salt, sugar; mix well. Add celery and stir-fry 3 to 4 minutes, until celery is crunchy but tender and still bright green. Keep warm until ready to serve.

Serves 4, more if other dishes are offered.

STIR-FRIED BEAN SPROUTS

A fast, simple extra dish for a Chinese meal.

1 16-ounce can bean
  sprouts
1 tablespoon oil

¼ teaspoon salt
½ teaspoon sugar
1 tablespoon soy sauce

1. Drain and rinse bean sprouts. Set ingredients by stove in order listed.
2. Set *wok* over medium-high heat for 30 seconds, swirl in to 30, add sprouts, stir-fry 1 minute. Add salt, sugar, soy sauce, and lower heat. Simmer 5 minutes, covered. Remove cover, stir-fry 1 minute more.

Serves 4, or more.

BRAISED PUMPKIN

Delicious, and handy for using jack-o'-lantern scrapings after Halloween. Nice with pork and chicken, Western-style, and with Eastern meals.

4 tablespoons pork or
  chicken fat, or oil
2 cups peeled, seeded
  pumpkin, shredded
½ stalk leek, or 1 teaspoon
  onion, minced

½ teaspoon salt
1 teaspoon sugar
1 teaspoon soy sauce
½ cup Chicken Stock

1. Measure fat, shred pumpkin on coarse side of grater. Prepare and measure all other ingredients and set by stove in order listed.
2. Set *wok* over medium high heat for 30 seconds, swirl in oil, count to 30, add pumpkin, stir-fry 3 minutes. Turn heat

to low, add leek, salt, sugar, soy sauce, stock; mix well, cover, simmer 8 to 10 minutes. Keep warm until ready to serve.
Serves 4 to 6.

STIR-FRIED ASPARAGUS, CELERY, SNOW PEAS, OR STRING BEANS

Stir-frying is a basic cooking method, and vegetables done this way can be flavored to suit your mood and the rest of the dinner—with the use of pork or chicken fat instead of oil; with the addition of a teaspoon or more of minced onion, scallion, or garlic; with the addition of sugar as well as salt; with the addition of soy sauce or oyster sauce, *Nuoc Mam* sauce when for Vietnamese dinners, and Japanese soy sauce when for Japanese dinners. Variations are endless. Experiment.

3 cups vegetable, cut in   2 tablespoons oil
   roll-cut diagonals   ½ teaspoon salt

1. Prepare vegetables and assemble ingredients by the stove.
2. Set *wok* over high heat for 30 seconds, add oil, count to 20, add vegetable pieces, stir and toss quickly to coat well with oil. Color will brighten in about 3 minutes or less of stir-frying. Add salt at this point; stir-fry another minute or so, and check for doneness. When color darkens and before it yellows, vegetables should be tender but still textured, and ready. They will finish cooking in their own heat. Serve as soon as possible.
Serves 6.

STIR-FRIED ONIONS OR SWEET PEPPERS

Cut 3 cups peeled onion or seeded washed pepper into rings ½ inch wide and stir-fry as for preceding recipe.

STIR-FRIED CABBAGE, LETTUCE, SPINACH, WATERCRESS, OR DANDELION

Any leafy green can be done this way. Remove tough stems that won't cook as quickly as green parts, slice them, and add to pan 1 minute before leafy portion goes in.

4 packed cups torn
  vegetable
2 tablespoons pork fat, or
  oil

½ teaspoon salt
¼ teaspoon sugar

1. Tear washed vegetable into leafy shreds, pack into cup and measure. Cut any large stalks into 1-inch pieces to cook 1 minute early, or discard.
2. Cook as Stir-fried Asparagus, for 2 to 3 minutes only, or until color is intense and leaves have wilted.
Serves 6.

STIR-FRIED CABBAGE, CARROTS, CAULIFLOWER, TURNIPS, OR WINTER SQUASH

Cabbage and turnips are nicest done in bacon fat or pork-roast drippings.

3 cups cut vegetable (see
  below)
2 tablespoons fat or oil
3 tablespoons water
½ teaspoon salt

1 teaspoon sugar (for
  cabbage and turnips
  only)
1 tablespoon soy sauce
  (optional)

1. Slice cabbage into thin shreds; grate carrots on coarse side of grater; cut cauliflower into smallest possible florets,

peel its stem, and slice into shreds ¼ inch thick and 1 inch long; grate turnips and various winter squashes the same as carrots. Place vegetable and other ingredients by stove in order listed.

2. Set *wok* over high heat for 30 seconds, swirl in fat, count to 30, add vegetable, and stir-fry 1 minute, coating well with fat. Add water, cover, and cook 8 to 10 minutes, or until vegetable is tender. Season with salt, sugar, and mix well before removing. Add soy sauce if you like.

Serves 6 or more.

STIR-FRIED SUMMER SQUASH, ZUCCHINI, TOMATOES, OR OKRA

Vegetables containing a lot of water can be done this way.

2 cups vegetable (see below)
1 tablespoon oil
1 clove garlic, peeled, smashed

½ teaspoon salt
Soy sauce, oyster sauce, or vinegar

1. Cut unpeeled squashes and zucchini into ¼-inch-thick rounds; cut tomatoes into medium wedges; break (don't cut) stems from okra; wash, place in boiling water for 1 minute, drain, dry, slice into thin rounds. Keep refrigerated until ready to cook. Gather ingredients by stove in order listed.

2. Set *wok* over high heat for 30 seconds, swirl in oil, count to 30, add garlic; stir-fry 1 minute. Add vegetable; toss well with oil. Add salt, cover, and cook 8 to 10 minutes, or until vegetable is tender. Flavor with soy, oyster sauce, or a little vinegar, to suit your taste.

Serves 6.

STIR-FRIED BROCCOLI

Delicious with any meaty dish.

1½ pounds broccoli, fresh
3 tablespoons oil
2 scallions, in 1-inch
   sections

½ teaspoon salt
½ teaspoon sugar
1 teaspoon soy sauce

1. Wash broccoli, break into small florets with some thin stem attached. Peel larger stems, cut into pieces ½ inch thick and 1 inch long. Measure and prepare other ingredients and set by stove.
2. Set *wok* over high heat for 30 seconds, swirl in oil, count to 20, add scallions and stir-fry ½ minute. Add broccoli and stir-fry until it turns very dark green. Add salt, sugar, soy sauce; stir once or twice, and serve at once.
Serves 6, more if other dishes are offered.

SWEET-AND-SOUR CARROTS

Good with roast pork and chicken, Western-style, too. Do shredded cabbage this way, or parsnips or sweet potatoes. Cube sweet potatoes.

1 tablespoon bacon fat, or
   oil
10 to 12 thin carrots, roll-
   cut in diagonals
1 cup water

2 tablespoons sugar
1 tablespoon cornstarch
2 tablespoons water
2 tablespoons vinegar
Salt to taste

1. Set prepared measured ingredients by stove in order listed, with sugar, cornstarch, water, vinegar, and salt mixed in a small bowl.

2. Set *wok* over medium-high heat for 30 seconds, swirl in fat, heat 20 seconds, add roll-cut carrot pieces and stir-fry 3 to 4 minutes. Add water, cover, simmer 5 minutes, until carrots are tender but not soft. When you hear sizzling, remove lid and test for readiness. A little liquid should remain in *wok* when carrots are ready. Push carrots to one side, pour cornstarch mixture down side of *wok*, stir until it thickens and clears. Stir in carrots. Can be kept warm until dinner is ready. Serves 4 to 6.

The Garnishes

MILD PEACH CHUTNEY

Pleasant, and the ingredients are readily obtained. Sterilize three 1-pint jars.

1⅔ cups sugar
1¾ cups cider vinegar
8 large peaches, peeled, sliced
7 sweet red peppers, seeded, chopped
3 medium onions, blender-chopped
1 clove garlic, peeled, minced

4 ounces candied ginger, chopped
1 teaspoon salt
1 cup seedless dark raisins
1 orange peel and pulp, chopped
1 lemon peel and pulp, chopped
⅔ cup almond halves, peeled
1 teaspoon ground ginger

1. Prepare and measure above ingredients; do peaches last so they won't darken.

2. In a preserving kettle over medium-high heat bring sugar and 1¼ cups of the vinegar to a boil and cook 5 minutes. Skim clear. Add peach slices, bring to a boil, simmer 10 minutes. Skim clear. Add peppers, onion, garlic, ginger, salt, raisins,

orange and lemon peel and pulp, and simmer 30 minutes, stirring frequently and skimming clear. Add almonds, ground ginger, and the remaining ½ cup vinegar. Cook 30 minutes more, stirring often to prevent sticking. Pour into sterilized pint jars, and seal.

Makes 3 pints.

MIXED-FRUIT CHUTNEY, INDIA

Yummy. Sterilize three 1-pint jars.

1⅔ cups sugar
1¾ cups cider vinegar
4 large peaches, peeled, sliced
2 ripe mangoes, sliced
1 cup pineapple chunks, drained
4 sweet red peppers, seeded, chopped
3 medium onions, blender-chopped

3 cloves garlic, peeled, minced
½ teaspoon cayenne powder
4 ounces candied ginger, chopped
1 cup seedless dark raisins
Peel ½ orange, slivered
Peel ½ lemon, slivered
½ cup almond halves, peeled
1 teaspoon ground ginger
½ teaspoon salt

Proceed as for Mild Peach Chutney, adding all fruit—peaches, mangoes, pineapple chunks—simultaneously.

RAITA

A side dish to offer with curries.

2 cucumbers, medium
1 onion, medium
½ teaspoon salt

½ teaspoon ground cumin
½ pint plain yogurt

Peel cucumber, grate on coarse side of grater, and set aside in refrigerator for 2 or 3 hours. Pour off cucumber juice, squeeze dry, cover with finely minced onion, and sprinkle with salt and cumin. Mix in yogurt, and let stand for 1 hour or more before serving.

Serves 6, or more.

ONION SAMBALL, INDIA

A side dish to offer with curries; allow 2 tablespoons per diner.

2 large onions
Salt to taste
4 tablespoons lemon juice, strained

Fresh mint leaves, or 1 drop spearmint

Mince onion fine, and salt to taste (I start with about 1½ teaspoons salt). Set in shallow bowl and sprinkle with lemon juice. Cover with fresh washed mint leaves. (Or mix 1 drop spearmint into lemon juice before adding.) Marinate 2 hours before serving.

Serves 8, or more.

SLICED COLD RADISH

Refreshing side dish with a Chinese flavor.

2 tablespoons vinegar
2 tablespoons soy sauce
1 tablespoon sugar

20 (1 bunch) fresh radishes
2 tablespoons sesame oil

1. Mix vinegar, soy sauce, sugar in blender briefly.
2. Wash radishes, remove tops and leaves, slice thinly on blade side of grater, or with a knife. Spread attractively on small round serving dish. Pour sauce over radish slices, chill

several hours, covered. Just before serving, sprinkle with sesame oil drops.

Serves 4, or more.

COLD AND SPICY CELERY, CUCUMBERS, OR ZUCCHINI

Chinese, and a delightful addition to a large, rich meal.

1 tablespoon oil	2 tablespoons vinegar
4 large celery stalks or 1	2 tablespoons soy sauce
medium cucumber or	1 tablespoon sugar
zucchini	Sesame oil

1. Measure oil. With potato peeler, cut washed, de-leafed celery into long thin strips; or cut unpeeled cucumber or zucchini into thinnest diagonal rounds. Blend vinegar, soy sauce, and sugar briefly.

2. Set *wok* over high heat for 30 seconds, swirl in oil, count to 30, add vegetables and stir-fry 1 minute only. Remove to serving plate, and mix lightly with vinegar mixture. Chill covered, for several hours, and before serving sprinkle with sesame oil.

Serves 4 to 6.

II. Sweets and Tea

DESSERTS ARE NOT a traditional part of Oriental meals. In India sweets once began the meal, and in China they are served with the rest of the meal. However, the Western custom of ending dinner with a sweet is pretty well established with most Americans (try skipping dessert with children around!), and we serve it in its appointed place.

The delightful Chinese lichees and kumquats, canned, and tart, fresh fruit such as chilled honeydew melon and pineapple (excellent together) go well with Oriental food and are no trouble to prepare. The Chilled Fruit Cream, India (below), is a nice addition to one's repertoire, and nutritious. Almond Cookies, traditional restaurant fare, are easy to make, and homemade Fortune Cookies provide fun at parties.

Tea does not normally end a Chinese meal. It is served between meals. However, tea is a correct beverage for Indian meals. Orange Pekoe, brewed 1 teaspoon to a cup and 1 for the pot, is the kind used in India generally, and it is served with sugar and milk.

At home we end Chinese meals with a China tea, often jasmine, brewed 1 heaping teaspoon to 6 cups of water, and sugar it lightly in the pot. Tea is best when the water used is beginning a rolling boil and the pot has been well scalded.

Tea is very closely related to the camellia, having similar fragrant flowers, and is sometimes grown for ornament. Black tea (for which the leaves have been fully fermented) is the strongest; green tea (unfermented) the lightest; and oolong (partially fermented) has a special flavor which some Westerners do not like. As an all-round tea, my household prefers an Indian-type, Earl Grey.

ALMOND COOKIES

Traditional ending to Chinese restaurant dinners, and a good dessert for parties since you can make them days ahead. Children don't like them, an advantage under most circumstances.

1½ cups all-purpose flour
½ teaspoon baking powder
¾ cup sugar
½ teaspoon salt
½ cup sesame oil, or butter
1 egg, slightly beaten

¼ cup skinned almonds, ground
½ teaspoon almond extract
18 to 25 blanched skinned almonds, whole
Egg white, slightly beaten (optional)

1. Measure flour, baking powder, sugar, salt into sifter, and sift once into medium bowl. Stir in oil and mix into dough (or cut in butter, as for pie crust). Add egg, add almonds ground in blender, add almond extract, and mix well.

2. Heat oven to 350°. Lightly grease and flour a cookie sheet. Scoop 1 tablespoon dough into your hand, roll between palms into a ball the size of a small walnut. If dough is too crumbly to roll, squeeze together until it adheres, then roll. Make all of the dough into balls. Place on cookie sheet 2 inches apart. Press whole blanched almond into each ball, squashing ball to about half its height. Brush with beaten egg white. Place in preheated oven, and bake about 16 minutes or until slightly browned. Cool. Store in airtight container.

Serves 8 to 15, makes 18 to 25 cookies.

FORTUNE COOKIES

A homemade version of the commercial product. Not much for flavor but they are great for family parties. A prediction children love reads: "Many precious gifts come with flying snow." They don't like: "Confucius say, swing high brings low grades." I like: "Stitch in time produces patched continuum," David's invention. Cakes should be hard, so make them days ahead.

3 eggs	½ teaspoon lemon extract
½ cup packed brown sugar	30 to 35 fortunes, small
½ cup all-purpose flour	

1. Beat eggs in electric mixer until frothy. Add sugar, flour, lemon extract and beat until thick. Set by stove with a pancake turner, a large platter, the folded fortunes, and a soup spoon.

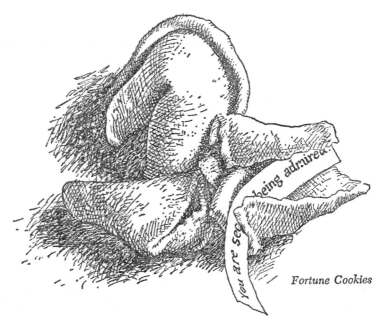

Fortune Cookies

2. Set heavy, flat griddle over medium heat and allow it to heat thoroughly. Spoon 3 blobs of batter onto the griddle and spread with spoon tip into 3-inch rounds. Cook only until dry enough to flip with spatula; turn, cook about ½ minute, and remove to platter. Lift pancake onto tips of thumb and first two fingers, poke a fortune gently into the cup formed, then press edges of pancake together firmly enough to seal. It may take a few tries before you get the knack. Cookie should look like a folded pancake bent in half. If you have trouble sealing, moisten edges with uncooked egg batter.

Makes about 30 cookies.

DATE WON-TONS

Delicious crunchy little pastries easy to make when you have a blender and the commercial Won-Ton Wrappers sold in specialty shops. Recipe for homemade wrappers is in Chapter 2.

8 ounces pitted dates
½ cup shelled walnuts
2 tablespoons orange juice, frozen
2 tablespoons grated orange rind

4 to 5 dozen Won-Ton Wrappers
3 cups oil
Confectioner's sugar

1. Cut dates into chunks about 1 inch square. Place in blender one quarter at a time, with one quarter of the walnuts. At high speed blend into finest particles. Turn into a large bowl, add orange juice and rind, and knead into a large ball. Roll into cylinders about 1 inch long, and fold and seal into Won-Ton Wrappers as illustrated.

2. Set *wok* over high heat for 30 seconds, swirl in oil and heat to 375° or until a day-old cube of bread browns (about 1

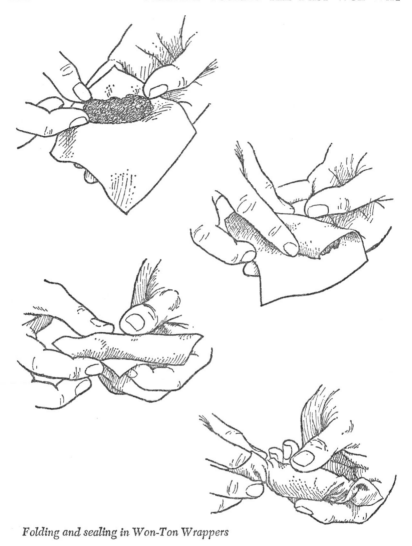

Folding and sealing in Won-Ton Wrappers

minute). Fry Won-Tons 6 to 8 at a time until just golden brown. Drain well on paper towel, cool, sprinkle lightly with confectioner's sugar before serving.

Serves 12 to 15, or more.

Eight Precious Pudding

EIGHT PRECIOUS PUDDING

A complex steamed rice pudding served on Chinese holidays. Glutinous rice and bean filling are sold at specialty shops.

1½ cups glutinous rice	12 blanched skinned
3½ cups water	almonds
½ cup water	1 cup red bean paste
1½ cups sugar	1 tablespoon cornstarch
12 pitted dates, halved	1½ cups water
24 dark seedless raisins	½ cup corn syrup
½ cup candied fruit,	½ cup sugar
chopped	

1. Simmer glutinous rice and 3½ cups water in a kettle with a tight-fitting lid until soft. Add ½ cup water and sugar; simmer 15 minutes more.

2. Oil sides and bottom of 1 large or 2 smaller molds and make a pattern of dates, raisins, candied fruit, and almonds along bottoms and sides. Pack bottoms and sides of molds with a layer of rice, gently, using about ⅔ of the quantity. Fill center with bean paste, and top with balance of rice. Seal molds with aluminum foil. Set molds on custard cups in a

large roasting pan that has a lid. Fill with 2 inches boiling water, set on 2 burners, cover, and steam puddings 1 hour, adding water as needed. Cool puddings, invert on serving dishes.

3. In a small saucepan simmer cornstarch mixed with water, corn syrup, and sugar until sauce thickens and clears. Serve hot over pudding.

Serves 12 or more.

FRIED ALMOND CUSTARD

Cornstarch dessert with an Eastern twist.

¼ cup sesame seeds	½ cup all-purpose flour
¼ cup sugar	1 tablespoon cornstarch
3 egg yolks	1 teaspoon almond extract
1 cup water	Cornstarch
2 tablespoons sugar	3 cups fresh oil

1. Over low heat in a heavy skillet, shake sesame seeds until they begin to turn golden. Remove to a sheet of brown paper, cover with another sheet of brown paper, and roll until cracked. Turn into a small bowl and mix with ½ cup sugar.

2. In blender at low speed combine egg yolks, water, sugar, flour, cornstarch, and almond extract. Turn into top of double boiler and stir over boiling water until mixture is very thick. Pour into 8-inch breadloaf pan, cool, cut into narrow 1-inch strips. Dredge strips in cornstarch.

3. When ready to serve, set *wok* over high heat for 30 seconds, swirl in oil, heat to 375° or until a day-old cube of bread browns (about 1 minute). Fry custard strips until lightly browned, 1 to 2 minutes, drain on paper towel. Sprinkle serving dish with ¼ sesame seed mixture, arrange fried custard on it, sprinkle liberally with remaining seeds.

Serves 6 or more.

PEKING DUST

Takes time, but is a gourmet's treat. To glacé walnuts combine 1½ cups sugar, ⅙ cup corn syrup, ¼ cup water, and a few grains of salt, and simmer to the hard-crack stage. Keep syrup hot over boiling water and dip nuts into it then drop onto an oiled cookie sheet and let harden.

4 cups raw chestnuts	1 cup heavy cream
2 tablespoons sugar	1 tangerine, or orange
Pinch salt	¼ cup glacéed walnuts

1. Gash chestnut tops, cover with water, boil 45 minutes. Shell, peel off inner skins, mash through ricer or sieve. Combine sugar and salt and mix into purée. Add more sugar if you like.

2. Whip cream until stiff, and fold ½ into chestnut purée. Taste, add more sugar if desired. Rinse a decorative mold in cold water, press purée gently into the mold. Chill 2 hours, turn into a serving dish, and cover with remaining whipped cream. Garnish with very thin orange slices and glacéed walnuts.

Serves 6 to 8, or more.

BANANAS IN A CANDY COAT

Fried bananas in a crackled candy coating with a Far Eastern flavor.

4 slightly green bananas	3 tablespoons cornstarch
2 tablespoons oil	½ teaspoon minced ginger,
1 teaspoon sugar	or ¼ teaspoon ground
⅔ cup cider vinegar	½ teaspoon salt
⅔ cup packed brown sugar	Large bowl of ice water

1. Peel bananas, halve down the length, halve again. Over medium heat, warm a heavy skillet, coat with oil, sprinkle with sugar, and lightly brown bananas. They should still be firm. In a small saucepan combine vinegar, brown sugar, cornstarch, and simmer until sauce thickens. Add ginger and salt, and simmer 4 minutes more. Return skillet to low heat, pour sauce over bananas and cook 2 minutes, basting constantly, coating each section thoroughly on all sides. Plunge sections 1 at a time into ice water long enough to harden candy coating, and set on a lightly oiled serving dish. Serve soon. Serves 4 to 8.

HONEYED APPLES

This is a dish to experiment with rather than something you will want to add to your everyday repertoire—but it is delicious and interesting.

3 tart medium apples	3 cups oil
2 egg whites, unbeaten	3 tablespoons fresh oil
2 tablespoons cornstarch	10 tablespoons sugar
2 tablespoons flour	1 tablespoon sesame seeds

1. Pare and core apples. Cut each into 8 pieces. Mix egg whites, cornstarch, and flour into lumpy batter. Add apples, and mix until each piece is coated. Set by the stove with a Chinese strainer or a slotted spoon. Place serving dish in oven at 250°, line dish with paper towel.

2. Set *wok* over high heat for 30 seconds, swirl in oil, heat to 350° or until a drop of batter sizzles and rises. Add pieces of apple 1 at a time, and fry in lots of 8 or 10 until golden brown. Drain on serving dish.

3. In a small saucepan, heat 3 tablespoons fresh oil, add

sugar, and stir over medium-low heat until sugar melts. Heat small griddle, stir and shake sesame seeds over medium heat until *light* golden brown. Add to oil and sugar mixture. Stir apple pieces in oil and sugar until each piece is glistening. Place on greased dish and serve hot, with a small glass dish containing water and ice. Dip apple slices in ice water before eating.

Serves 3 to 6.

BANANA HALVAH, INDIA

A cooked-fruit dessert that goes well with any meal.

5 bananas
2 tablespoons butter
1 cup water
¾ cup sugar
1 teaspoon frozen orange
    juice

4 tablespoons sliced
    almonds
1 teaspoon ground peeled
    cardamom seeds

Peel bananas, cut into 1-inch sections. In a heavy enameled skillet over medium heat melt butter and sauté bananas 5 minutes, stirring. Lower heat, remove skillet, and mash bananas. Return skillet to fire, mix in ½ cup water, stirring constantly. Stir in sugar. As ingredients dry, beat in remaining water. Simmer 20 minutes, stirring occasionally. Add orange juice, stir 1 more minute, pour into sherbet glasses and chill. Serve sprinkled with almonds and ground cardamom.

Serves 4 to 6.

CHILLED FRUIT CREAM, INDIA

Sweetened yogurt and sour cream with fruit and nuts—no trouble whatever and made in a few minutes.

1 pint vanilla yogurt
1 pint sour cream
½ cup sugar
⅛ teaspoon saffron
  (optional)

½ cup drained crushed
  pineapple, or wild
  strawberries
1 tablespoon almond slices

In a large bowl mix yogurt into sour cream with sugar and saffron. Fold in ¾ths of the fruit and nuts. Scoop into serving dish or sherbet glasses, decorate with remaining fruit and nuts.

Serves 8 to 12.

12. Six Dishes for Dieters

CHINESE AND most other Oriental meals are lower in calories and usually higher in the relative proportion of vegetables than are Western meals. If you skip the rice and halve the oil, a good many Chinese meals will be ideal for dieters. The following recipes are especially for persons who are watching their weight or cholesterol count.

CRAB WITH ALMONDS, CELERY, AND MUSHROOMS

Crunchy crab concoction with almond bits and celery for texture. Nice with plain rice and spinach stir-fried with garlic. Nice with Beef Shreds with Onions, too. I use 2 or 3 packages of frozen Alaska King crab to make this, unless we are at the shore.

½ cup toasted almond slices
1 pound raw crabmeat
1 tablespoon cornstarch
½ cup Chicken Stock
1 tablespoon oil
1 clove garlic, peeled, smashed
1 teaspoon salt
1 slice fresh ginger, ⅛ inch thick, minced
1 cup mushroom slices, ⅛ inch thick
3 stalks celery, diced (1 cup)
1 teaspoon soy sauce
½ teaspoon sugar
1 teaspoon sherry

1. Toast almond slices in a few drops of oil over medium heat in a heavy skillet until golden. Shape crabmeat into cubes about 1 inch square. Mix cornstarch with Chicken Stock. Set all ingredients in order listed by the stove.

2. Set *wok* over high heat for 30 seconds, swirl in oil, count to 30, add garlic, salt, ginger; stir-fry a few *seconds;* add mushroom slices and stir-fry 1 minute. Add celery; stir-fry 1 minute more. Add toasted almonds, crab, soy sauce, and sugar. Sprinkle with sherry, and stir-fry gently to avoid shredding crab, 3 minutes. Push ingredients to one side, dribble cornstarch mixture down side of *wok*, and stir until sauce clears and thickens. Mix all ingredients, serve at once. Offer soy sauce at table. Serves 4, more if other dishes are offered.

VEGETABLE CHOP SUEY

Crunchy, pretty, and mildly flavored. Make it into a late-summer chop suey by substituting scallions, cucumber, tomatoes, green peppers for vegetables here, and serve on shredded lettuce.

2 tablespoons oil	3 green onions, minced
¼ cup lean pork shreds, cooked or raw	½ cup bean sprouts, rinsed
½ cup Chinese cabbage, or plain cabbage, shredded	1 cup Beef Stock
	½ teaspoon salt
¼ cup celery, in ½-inch-thick rounds	2 tablespoons soy sauce
	1 tablespoon cornstarch
1 green pepper, shredded	3 tablespoons water

1. Prepare ingredients as listed, mixing cornstarch with 3 tablespoons water, and set by the stove in order listed.

2. Set *wok* over high heat for 30 seconds, swirl in oil, count to 30, add pork shreds, and stir-fry ½ minute. Add cabbage; stir-fry ½ minute. Add celery; stir-fry ½ minute. Add pepper and onion, and stir-fry ½ minute. Add bean sprouts; stir-fry 3

minutes more. Push ingredients to one side, pour Beef Stock down side of *wok*. Season with salt and soy sauce. When simmering, add cornstarch mixture. Stir until sauce clears; mix with solid ingredients; serve at once.

Serves 4 to 6, more if other dishes are offered.

CHICKEN, SHRIMP, AND VEGETABLES, JAPAN

This is a pretty dish, cooked entirely in stock, without fat or oil of any kind.

1 cup water
4 tablespoons soy sauce
  (Kikkoman)
3 tablespoons sugar
½ teaspoon salt
½ cup raw shrimp, shelled,
  deveined

1 package frozen snow
  peas
4 tablespoons dry sherry
1½ pounds chicken
1 package frozen asparagus
6 dried Chinese mushrooms

1. In a bowl combine water, 3 tablespoons soy sauce, sugar, and salt. Thaw shrimp and snow peas. Measure sherry. Skin and bone chicken and cut into pieces the size and shape of the snow peas. Measure 1 tablespoon soy sauce. Thaw asparagus. Cover mushrooms with boiling water, soak 20 minutes, drain, reserving ½ cup liquid. Set all ingredients by the stove in the order listed.

2. Set heat at high, add water mixture to *wok* or a kettle, and bring to a boil. Add shrimp and boil until pink and opaque. Remove with slotted spoon to a serving dish. Add snow peas; bring to a boil; add sherry and chicken; stir and cook about 5 minutes. Remove to serving dish and sprinkle with 1 tablespoon soy sauce. If water is low, add a little of the mushroom liquid. Add asparagus and mushrooms, cook 3 to 4 minutes, and remove to serving dish. Arrange all ingredients separately and decoratively on the platter, and serve with a little of the cooking liquid.

Serves 6.

BAKED CHICKEN

3 to 4 pounds chicken
1 tablespoon dry sherry
2 tablespoons soy sauce
½ teaspoon sugar

½ small sweet onion
1 teaspoon powdered
   ginger

1. Heat oven to 450°.
2. Cut boned chicken into pieces 1 inch long and ⅛ inch thick across the grain. (Save the bones and skin for soup.) Mix sherry, soy sauce, sugar, onion, and ginger in a bowl. Pour mixture over the chicken and marinate for 15 minutes. Divide chicken into 8 portions and wrap each portion in a 12-inch square of aluminum foil, keeping seams up. Bake 6 minutes, and serve without rice.
   Serves 6 to 8.

STEAK WITH GARLIC

Delicious, if you like garlic, but not for anyone allergic to it. Serve with plain rice, or without, and a multiple vegetable dish.

1 pound boneless sirloin
2 tablespoons soy sauce
1 tablespoon hoisin sauce,
   or extra soy sauce
2 tablespoons dry sherry

1½ teaspoons sugar
4 cloves garlic, peeled,
   sliced
3 tablespoons oil

1. Cut sirloin against the grain into slices 2 inches long by 1 inch wide by ¼ inch thick. Set on platter exposing one side of each piece. Cover with mixture of soy sauce, hoisin sauce, and sherry. Sprinkle with sugar. Arrange thin garlic slices over

steak. Marinate 1 hour or more at room temperature. Set by stove with oil and slotted spoon.

2. Set *wok* over highest heat for 30 seconds, swirl in oil, heat to almost smoking, remove beef from marinade with slotted spoon. Reserve marinade. Stir-fry steak quickly for 2 minutes. After 1½ minutes, pour remaining marinade over steak so that it finishes cooking in marinade. Serve at once. Serves 4.

SCALLOPS WITH MUSHROOMS

Wonderfully fast and tasty seafood dish, which acquires a Western accent if you substitute butter for oil, and season with lemon juice instead of soy. Makes a fine Lenten one-dish dinner with rice.

2 tablespoons oil	2 tablespoons soy sauce
2 to 3 cups raw scallops	1 teaspoon salt
½ pound mushrooms	1 teaspoon sugar
1 scallion	
1 teaspoon fresh minced ginger, or ½ teaspoon ground	

1. Measure oil. Rinse scallops and drain well; if large, halve. Wipe mushrooms and slice into lengths ⅛ inch thick. Cut scallion into 1-inch sections. Place with all other ingredients by the stove in the order listed.

2. Set *wok* over high heat for 30 seconds, swirl in oil, count to 20. Add scallops; stir-fry 5 minutes. Add mushrooms, scallion, ginger, soy sauce, salt, and sugar. Stir-fry 2 minutes more. Serve hot.

Serves 4 to 6, more if other dishes are offered.

Where to Buy

Many larger cities in the United States now have one or more shops carrying Oriental cooking utensils and/or imported foods. Consult the classified directory of the large city nearest to you. Or send your inquiry to one of the following list of suppliers. Most of these concerns will accept mail orders.

Boston:

Legal Sea Foods Market
237 Hampshire Street
Cambridge, Mass. 02139
Equipment and food.

Wing Wing Imported Groceries
79 Harrison Avenue
Boston, Mass. 02111
Equipment and food; catalogue available.

Washington, D.C.:

Mee Wah Lung Company
608 H Street, N.W.
Washington, D.C.
No mail orders.

New York:

Eastern Trading Company
2801 Broadway
New York, N.Y. 10025
Equipment and food.

Katagiri and Company
224 East 59th Street
New York, N.Y. 10022
Sell *woks* and food; catalogue available.

Yuet Hing Market, Inc.
23 Pell Street
New York, N.Y. 10013
Equipment and food; catalogue available.

Chicago:

Kam Shing Company
2246 South Wentworth Street
Chicago, Ill. 60616
Equipment and food; mail orders of $10 and more; catalogue available.

Shiroma
1058 West Argyle Street
Chicago, Ill. 60640
Equipment and food; catalogue available.

Star Market
3349 North Clark Street
Chicago, Ill. 60657
Equipment and food.

Texas:

Oriental Import-Export Company
2009 Polk Street
Houston, Tex. 77002
Equipment and food; price list available.

California:

Mow Lee Sing Kee Company
774 Commercial Street
San Francisco, Calif. 94108
Sell equipment and food.

Wing Chong Lung Company
922 South San Pedro Street
Los Angeles, Calif. 90015
Carry cooking equipment and food; catalogue available soon.

Index

Menus from the Orient

Indian Dinner for Six

Shrimp Balls, India
Lamb Korma, India
Chutney   Raita
Rice   Diced Apples
Banana Halvah, India

Indian Patio Party for Eight

Pakoras
Chicken Pulao with Shrimp, India
Beef Kebabs
Shredded Coconut   Raita
Chutney   Onion Samball, India
Chilled Fruit Cream, India

Indian Luncheon for Two or Four

Mulligatawny, India
Egg Curry, India
Chutney   Onion Samball, India
Vanilla Yogurt

Japanese Dinner for Eight

Japanese Egg Rolls
Sukiyaki
Rice   Chilled Radish Slices
Raw Grated Baby Turnips
Chilled Mandarin Oranges (canned)

Japanese Patio Dinner for Six

Vegetable Soup, Japan
Sashimi (Raw Fish), Japan
Vinegared Rice, Japan
Tempura Dinner, Japan
Honeydew Melon and Lime Juice

Vietnamese Dinner for Eight

Vegetable Soup, Japan
Pastry Rolls, Vietnam
Fu Yung, Vietnam
Chicken and Tomatoes Stir-Fried,
    Vietnam
Pot-Fried Rice, Vietnam or Rice
Vegetable Mix, Vietnam
Pineapple and Melon Fruit Cup

Vietnamese Dinner for Six

Eggs with Cabbage, Vietnam
Meat Loaf, Vietnam
Green Beans and Shrimp, Vietnam
Tomato Slices with Chives
Honeyed Apples

Javanese Dinner for Six

Pakoras or Shrimp Tempura
Chicken and Fruit Curry, Java
Grated Coconut   Diced Apples
Rice   Sliced Tomatoes
Chilled Fruit Cream, India

Siamese Dinner for Two

Spice Sauce with Fish Chunks, Siam
Rice   Raita
Fried Almond Custard

Malaysian Dinner for Six

Pakoras
Chicken with Fruit and Almonds,
    Malaysia
Grated Coconut   Chutney
Rice   Sliced Tomatoes and
    Cucumbers
Yogurt with Sliced Sweetened
    Strawberries

Burmese Dinner for Four

Fish Balls, Burma
Rice   Chutney
Onion Samball, India
Vanilla Yogurt with Crushed
    Pineapple